THE CAREER TRAP

Other Books by Jeffrey G. Allen

THE CAREER TRAP

Breaking Through the
10-Year Barrier
to Get the Job
You Really Want

Jeffrey G. Allen, J.D., C.P.C.

amacom

American Management Association

New York • Atlanta • Boston • Chicago • Kansas City • San Francisco • Washington, D.C.
Brussels • Mexico City • Tokyo • Toronto

Library of Congress Cataloging-in-Publication Data

Allen, Jeffrey G., 1943–
        The career trap : breaking through the 10-year barrier to get the
    job you really want / Jeffrey G. Allen.
            p.   cm.
        Includes bibliographical references and index.
        ISBN 0-8144-7823-9
        1. Career changes.   2. Career plateaus.   3. Vocational guidance.
    I.   Title.
    HF5383.A45   1995
    650.14 —dc20   95-780
                                                                    CIP

321.7
A 427c

Printing number

10   9   8   7   6   5   4   3   2   1

Contents

— 12 **How to Become Relentlessly Recruited**

Executive recruiting has gone through drastic changes in the last decade. Factors that increase your visibility will do wonders for your hireability. And once you're on the headhunters' roster of up-and-comers, it's like having a top Hollywood agent screening properties for your next starring role.

13 **Building a Network to Get Work**

Keep all your options open—job clubs, trade associations, community groups, and those informal contacts. An active Rolodex is the essential key.

— 14 **Keeping Your Job Until You're Ready to Leave**

A time will come when that coveted new position loses its luster. Even if the decision to leave isn't yours, you can cushion the blow with a separation file and a severance package.

15 **Conclusion**

Making the ten-year career change can provide you with an excellent opportunity to increase your potential worth to an employer. Whatever lies ahead, you're now ready to apply this proven systematic approach to the rest—and best years—of your career.

Acknowledgments

With appreciation . . .

To my wife, **Bev;**
to my son, **Rick;**
to an editor's editor, **Mary Glenn;**
and to **Harriet Modler,** the most capable
   assistant any author could want.

Thanks more than words can say.

THE CAREER TRAP

Chapter 1

Career Stalls: The What and Why

If you're bored at work, frustrated by repetition, and feeling unappreciated by management, you could be in the middle of first-decade meltdown. When you started your career in the middle of the frenetic 1980s, conspicuous consumption was the order of the day. Armed with your degree, or at least your youthful ambitions, you marched into the business world.

A decade later enthusiasm has been replaced by futility. You may feel forever locked into midmanagement mediocrity. On the one hand you're tormented by fears of corporate downsizing or the eroding obsolescence of your skills. On the other, you realize you can't stay locked into this position forever.

The Time Telescope

Andy Warhol's famous remark about everyone reaching for his "fifteen minutes of fame" fits you too. You're not even famous, but it seems as if your glory days or fifteen minutes of opportunity have passed you by, even before your career has peaked.

Add to this a feeling that time is speeding up, going by faster and faster. You see it everywhere—cycles that once took thirty years to evolve now come and go in less than ten. What happened over the span of a decade is now recycled in a fashion season of three months, like bell-bottoms from the 1970s or punk rock from the 1980s. TV news is thirty-second sound bites and MTV images flash by in nanoseconds.

On top of it all, before moving into this midthirties meltdown, didn't it seem as if the remainder of your career life would be infinite?

Now you wonder how it could have gone by so fast and what you are going to do about the future.

Do You Live to Work or Work to Live?

Contrary to the pop psychology books that stress personal identity, most professionals feel their strongest self-worth centers around what they do for a living. Work meets our most deeply rooted psychological needs. It's the cornerstone of our identities. It's all tied up with our sense of self-esteem, status, control of our lives, even our understanding of the world.

Until the socially conscious 1960s, the main reason for the average Joe to work was simply to receive a paycheck. That all began to change when baby boomers received extended liberal educations and reaped the bounty of economic security. After that, careers became enmeshed with upward mobility, success, and personal gratification.

A Gallup poll taken near the end of the 1980s found that Americans whose work gave them a sense of identity worked harder and more contentedly than those who punched a time clock. Seventy percent of interviewees in another recent study said they would continue to work even if they didn't need a paycheck. You see stories like this periodically when a multimillionaire is born by winning a lottery. One man who won part of the California lottery and will receive $70,000 after taxes for the next twenty years is still working at his same job in the Veterans Administration. But he's in the minority. According to that study, only 39 percent would stay in their *same* job.

In 1993 the *Los Angeles Times* reported that a survey by the Families and Work Institute in New York found that 82 percent of Americans defined success in work as "the personal satisfaction gained from doing a good job or earning the respect of supervisors and peers. Only 21 percent listed making a good income as the definition of success."* Of all the employees who switched jobs in the previous five years their main reasons for choosing a new employer were open communications, the effect of the job on personal and family life, the nature of the work, quality of management, and characteristics of supervisors. Salary was in a distant sixteenth place.

The Dilemma of Downward Mobility

Given the economic angst of the 1990s, you can't afford to be totally unconcerned about salary. Money is still the bottom line.

*All references are listed in the Bibliography.

Latter-day baby boomers are the first generation since the 1980s that have not done better than the generation that preceded it. You've been conditioned to expect to move ahead—everyone else did. Why can't you? Combining the long-term effects of inflation since the 1970s with the upward bracket creep of taxes you discover that the salaries of liberal arts graduates of the 1980s are 30 percent to 35 percent less in real income than those who began their careers in 1970.

Faced with these depressing realities, midthirties meltdown occurs in predictable stages: overload and stagnation followed by frayed emotions and, if not handled properly, full-scale burnout including apathy, hopelessness, and helplessness. Most people who have been with one employer for ten years tend to lose confidence in their own adaptability. (Yet, within three months after making a change, people are usually amazed at just how easily the transition went.)

The Plateauing Factor

You can't be too hard on yourself when you realize that your professional and economic status also has its roots in the era when you were born. Author Judith Bardwick in *The Plateauing Trap* defines plateauing as the inability to rise to levels in which you would be competent. It's the exact opposite of the Peter Principle made famous in the late 1950s and early 1960s, where managers were "kicked upstairs" into jobs in which they had no skills due to a lack of excecutive talent. These people had the good luck to be born during the low-birth years of the depression and World War II.

You're stuck in the lower or middle ranks of management because there is greater competition for fewer jobs at the top. In the 1950s there were plenty of jobs to go around. By the 1980s, with the huge birth rates of the baby boomers, there were thirty candidates for each job. Fran Schumer wrote in "Downward Mobility" published in *New York* magazine "There are quite simply too many people in the same cohort" (meaning ten-year age group).

When you entered management a decade ago, it wasn't uncommon to change jobs every eighteen to twenty-four months. If you looked especially promising, you might have been started on the fast track. As you moved up, you also slowed down, because there are far fewer obvious positions and far too many people crowding to get them.

It's Time for a Shake-Up—Psychological and Professional

You're far more likely than your parents to act on value shifts. Not only can you conceive of changing jobs, but perhaps even careers. In

1988 a Gallup poll reported that 25 percent of all Americans between ages twenty-six and forty were planning on changing jobs or careers within three years.

You don't have to settle for "good enough." You live in a time when it's not only possible, but necessary, to reinvent yourself. You can do it. Why? Because job changing success depends 70 percent on specific job-hunting skills and only 30 percent on previous background and ability. You have the latter, and in this book I will show you my own proven tricks of the trade for the former.

What's more, you even have the edge over younger competition, because knowing where you went wrong is at least as important as what you did right. I once knew a woman who created a successful employment agency. She was so good she soon had many copying her techniques. But she wasn't worried. "Why should I be?" she asked me. "I've already learned from my mistakes; they still have to make them."

By combining the road map to successful job hunting in the following chapters with your own subtlety of experience, you can make it.

Chapter 2

The Ten-Year Career Barrier

Before you can give your career and paycheck a boost, let's analyze what's holding you back. Maybe it's financial and family obligations, a variety of psychological changes, or even your perceptions about aging at work.

Established Standard of Living

Ten years ago, financial expectations were different. Yuppies were in vogue and upward financial mobility appeared limitless. Now, things have changed. Although your parents could raise you and your siblings on a single paycheck and put some money away for your education and that proverbial rainy day, now it takes two working adults to finance a lifestyle of limited comforts.

There's even a name for an uncomfortable new phenomenon. Does it fit you? In *Fortysomething*, Ross Goldstein, Ph.D., and Diana Landau wrote about the middle-aged downwardly mobile urban professional or MADMUP. Considerable unemployment is all around you—like the documented case of twenty-three K-Mart managers fired because of their age and high salaries. In a TV report on the case ("Eye to Eye," October 18, 1993, on CBS), one manager said, "I went from a lucrative lifestyle to near poverty."

Even if your income has not taken a downturn, just finding that you've topped out in your present job gives no sense of satisfaction. It's just a dead end.

In most middle- and high-income communities, money is what dictates who socializes and whether your kids go to private school. Knowing that can either increase your frustration or rekindle your ambition. It's not the only driving force. But it's a powerful one.

5

Routine Lifestyle

Is conspicuous consumption your economic weakness? Are you what you wear, where you dine? People don't like to admit to such shallow tendencies, but one of the most obvious frustrations we face is that possessions become a sign of personal worth.

Round and round you go, spending money so people know you have it while your security goes down the toilet. Throwing money around is almost like a drug. People cater to you when they perceive that you have money, and it feels good.

I went out with some friends who have a new Jaguar; it was parked in the place of honor at a restaurant. Driving up in my family sedan, I didn't rate a second look. When your salary's good, it's hard to climb the mental mountain that puts you in the mood to look for a new position—even if your current job is stifling you.

Fixed Expenses

Charting fixed expenses give you a realistic perspective. You might decide it's too risky to make a move now. On the other hand, you might find that your savings can cushion your search for a better position.

First, list essential expenditures such as food, utilities, mortgage, and health insurance. Then add other obligations such as car and loan payments or credit card bills. Next itemize the expenditures required during your job-hunting efforts—for quality resumes, good stationery, new business clothes, more frequent trips to the hairdresser. Finished with the must-haves? Now see where you can make the deepest cuts in discretionary spending, such as entertainment and dining out.

Increased Family Expenses

From the time middle-class children are infants, they're required to be on a kiddie fast track if their parents happen to be on the adult version. Parents are caught up in the enrichment frenzy—personal computer toys to stimulate the baby's mind, infant designer fashions, even toddler gyms. Later on, it's karate or dance lessons. In addition to the traditional braces, now a nose job may be essential for your teenage daughter's feeling of self-worth. Especially in large cities, where public schools were perfectly acceptable a decade ago, now no right-thinking parent would entrust a child's education to anything but a private school whose graduates routinely matriculate to Harvard.

If you're working ever harder to pay for all these must-haves, it becomes a vicious cycle. You are away from home making the money to buy the goodies; then you feel guilty for staying away, so you buy more and pile up more credit card charges.

Relationships With Colleagues and Friends

Holding on to a long-term job takes its emotional toll, particularly if the job has lost its challenge. Maybe you conquered it a long time ago and are now going through the motions. You must weigh risking the great unknown against perceived security. Many of today's businesses actually reward mobility over long-term fidelity.

That aura over the head of the new person in your department is the new boy/new girl halo effect. If it's been years since your last promotion, management may see you as fresh out of ideas or on a dead-end track. If you're suffering benign neglect in a longtime job, you wind up with little opportunity to give input on major decisions. Your performance evaluations are infrequent and usually perfunctory. Your peers, subordinates, and superiors may well look through you, like the proverbial man who wasn't there.

If promotion is your personal priority and you're passed over, you're going to internalize it. "It means they preferred Joe to me," your psyche says, and that really hurts.

> I evaluate myself against all the people who have those other, higher jobs. It's me against them. When I'm not chosen, I want to know in what way they are better than me. Only a promotion counts; all other forms of praise are easy. I want to see that the higher-ups really believe that in some ways, I'm as good as the rest. . . ."

wrote Judith Bardwick of a manager frustrated with his lack of progress in *The Plateauing Trap*. Since work is so closely linked to our egos, it is not merely something we do to make a living. It is who we are. When that coveted promotion goes to Joe instead of you, it can shake the very foundation of your self-worth.

Be careful. While you're nursing your wounds, at least be discreet. Otherwise, you can risk alienating friends and valuable business contacts. Too much overt angst makes them feel threatened. Try to pick listeners who have been there. Like any other support group, letting it all hang out works best when you confide in people who have gone through similar problems and survived.

Meeting Your Family Responsibilities

"Certainly the family unit operates from a much better position to turn the screws than a casual acquaintance or even a close friend," observed Donald G. Smith in . . . *And They Also Kick You When You're Down.* Unless you have an iron will and resolve to keep work and home totally separate, conflicts at work usually spill over into frustrations at home.

When promotions go to someone else, one typical reaction is to prove your importance at work by bringing more work home. You spend less time in family activities and haven't a clue what your family's doing. With a growing family and increasing expenses, you begin to resent your family. Then you feel guilty. The next stage is fatigue, complete with frayed tempers, all around. Even your sex life suffers.

If you're a woman, you face additional pressures. You're either being sidelined on the mommy track or feeling guilty over spending too much time at work. The glass ceiling may also limit your professional progress. What can you do to keep the guilt–exhaustion syndrome at bay while you figure out your next professional move? Just let your family know what you're going through. Small kids may not understand it. But they may be sympathetic if you simply say, "I'm really not mad at you—Mommy just had a bad day at work." Telling your spouse that you realize that you're in a rotten frame of mind can also make life more bearable. Your family may not enjoy your companionship right now, but at least they know where you're coming from.

Coping With Older Parents

Living longer is a double-edged sword. If your parents had you when they were older, you may be partially or totally responsible for managing their physical care or finances. Four out of five disabled elderly in the United States are cared for by relatives, 75 percent by their daughters. In 1990, there were 31 million people over age sixty-five in the United States. That's 12.5 percent of the population. Medicare spends more than $145 billion a year on health care for the elderly. By the time you reach that age, 20 percent of the population will be old, and the costs are projected at a stunning $4.1 trillion annually!

Even if your parents aren't financially dependent on you, you face a lot of guilt, especially if you live far away from them. Ours is the first generation to move a nuclear family, almost at will, virtually anywhere in response to job requirements. If you remain close by your parents, your emotions may run the gamut of fear, anger, sorrow, and more guilt as you see reminders of your own morality. How can your once strong parents now be so weak and infirm?

There's a lot of similarity between your parents and your adolescent children. Both want you and don't want you; both need you and don't like to admit it. All the while, you're juggling responsibilities for both generations.

You may be confused at this role reversal for your parents as they now become dependent on you for transportation, food, shelter, clothing, and companionship. This reversal even extends to financial considerations. Your income is still climbing (you hope) while theirs is fixed or perilously declining. If you have to help them financially, the crunch is doubled as you try to save for the kids' college funds and help pay for Dad's hearing aid or Mom's dental work. "But what about me?" you ask, plaintively. When is there ever going to be enough time to spend with my family, enjoying myself. Or what about a romantic trip for the two of us?

The bad news is coping with a confusing array of conflicting emotions can take its toll on your family and parents. On the brighter side, now as never before there are more gerontology specialists, health resource centers, and psychological services dedicated to assisting the aged and the people who care for them.

Competing With Younger Employees

In addition to all the financial and emotional baggage you're carrying, there's still the overriding concern about how you look to the people you work with. Everyone is judged within a promotional window of opportunity, and age-related comparisons are inevitable. "They" think if you're a few years older, you're less creative, less enthusiastic than you were, even five years ago. Once you sense this attitude in coworkers and superiors, you're at risk for letting it become a self-fulfilling prophecy.

The truth is not that you're suddenly too old but that you've been in the same job for too long. And it's equally true for pay raises.

In a 1993 *Los Angeles Times* feature "Making All You're Worth," Noeleta Lacey, founder of Lacey Shorthand Reporting Corporation, pointed out that "the high flying spending of the 1980s is over. Today, to get a raise you've got to earn your keep. If someone is really on the ball, with an incredible awareness of company needs and ideas for cost-saving techniques, they should speak up and they will be rewarded."

The obvious solution is not to work harder but to work smarter. Unfortunately that does not usually happen. Reacting to your perceived loss of corporate importance, you may retreat to workaholism, which ultimately leads to the family frustrations mentioned earlier.

If you see yourself in this scenario, there are two questions to ask:

1. How long can I realistically continue to work at this pace?
2. Am I doing this to drown out my overall discontent?

Before your stamina gives out and your frustrations become impossible to live with, you must choose between simply living with the situation or starting a new job search. You're always in a better position to start the process when you're employed than after pink-slip time.

Interacting With Younger Employees

In place of the boundless energy you once possessed, you start to feel tired earlier. It's frustrating, especially when the new faces at work are never pooped at the end of the day. Remember that they may be more energetic, but that doesn't make them more efficient. You've got the experience when it comes to productively managing your time.

What's even more galling is when people only seven to ten years younger than you start to act as if you're from a whole earlier generation. The inferences may appear in a kidding reference to "Pops," or in offering to pick up a heavy object for you. On your coffee breaks, you may discover your coworkers are talking about music groups you never knew existed.

One of the best ways to dispel this stigma is to create the respect that supplants ageism. Let them know lightly but firmly that you're up to anything they can throw at you.

When your department gets a new supervisor who's years younger than you, it's another rude slap in the face. Your initial reaction may be outrage and hurt.

To stay where you are means you must make age a nonissue and forget your prejudices. Not so easy. But if you're going to stay in that job, facilitating your new supervisor's success is the best way to enhance yours.

How to Tell If You're Locked In to the Slow Track

In *Unwritten Rules for Your Career*, George B. Graen studied two hundred managers and their supervisors as they built new teams following a major corporate restructuring. All bosses and managers were interviewed during the first, fourth, seventh, and ninth months.

Four months into the job, the slow-trackers had these complaints:

- Problems getting needed information
- No involvement in major decisions
- Difficulty getting responses from their bosses
- Reluctance of their bosses to smooth the way for them or bail them out of negative situations

For the fast-trackers, the results were just the opposite:

- When procedures were changed, they were among the first to know.
- They often participated in discussions of projected changes.
- Bosses supported their actions and helped negotiate tricky areas.
- Work relations with supervisors and coworkers were positive.
- They were required to perform less routine work.

What separates these two groups is the relationships with their direct supervisors. Supervisor/manager negotiations for the fast-trackers weren't formalized; they became part of the unwritten corporate codes.

If you recognize yourself in the first group, standing outside with your nose pressed to the glass wondering what went wrong, you need a change.

Chapter 3

The Legality and Reality of Age Discrimination

As you near the Big 4-0, you start to pay more attention to things you never considered a decade ago—like health insurance and retirement. Today's aging baby boomers make a disproportionate statistical bulge in the lineup for benefits.

The Age Discrimination in Employment Act

As you climb the corporate ladder, your salary increases and retirement benefits add up—things that downsizing corporations are shunning like the plague. That's the downside. The upside is that with the aging of America has come the only truly significant piece of national legislation to address worker needs: The Age Discrimination Employment Act of 1967 (ADEA) and its 1974 extension. In a way it's your safety net, since age cannot be the overt basis for dismissal. But that hasn't stopped overzealous employers and their cadre of attorneys from trying to ease out costly older workers through the loopholes. Before you decide whether to stay where you are or move on, you'd better bone up on the law.

One fact is clear—the older you are, the longer it takes to find a new job. In 1987 the U.S. Department of Labor, Bureau of Labor Statistics reported that it took 12.5 weeks for a person between ages twenty and twenty-four to find a new job; for people between the ages of thirty-five and forty-four, it was 18.2 weeks, or nearly 50 percent longer!

Who Is Covered

Federal law includes ages forty through seventy for all private enterprises with twenty or more employees, all federal and local governments, labor unions, even the activities of employment agencies, executive recruiters, and others who find work for others as being covered under this statute. Although age seventy is the upper limit for the national statute, some states have expanded protection to include any age discrimination.

Provisions

- Prohibits discrimination in hiring, retaining a job, wages and salaries, fringe benefits, and perquisites.
- Prohibits advertising that excludes women and older workers.
- Permits early retirement incentives but prohibits forced retirement.
- Prohibits forced retirement due to disability, if you can show that you can still do the job.

Related Discriminatory Criteria

- Expressly precludes liability for discharge based "on a factor other than age" or for "good cause." This is a gaping chasm in your protection.
- Excludes any situation where age is a bona fide occupational qualification (e.g., where strength or split-second alertness is a necessity in such occupations as firefighting, police work, or piloting an airplane).
- Permits use of an age-based seniority system (e.g., union jobs).
- Permits mandatory retirement of policy makers and executives at age sixty-five.

Provisions for Enforcement

- Remedy cannot be undertaken as a general class action suit.
- A more limited form of class action is permitted under provisions of the Fair Labor Standards Act where persons can become members of the litigating class only by taking affirmative steps to opt in. You specifically must take a positive action to be included in a group.
- The plaintiff must show sufficient evidence from which a jury can infer that age was a determining factor in the employer's decision. If you make such a case, the employer has the burden of producing evidence to show that adverse employment action was taken for a legitimate, nondiscriminatory reason. Then it's again up to you to show that this reason is merely a pretext for

your dismissal. The bottom line? You, the employee, carry the burden of persuasion.

- Action may be brought by a private individual or the government.
- There are no specific time limits for attempts at conciliation.
- Individuals may not sue until they first file with the Equal Employment Opportunity Commission (EEOC) or proper state agency with jurisdiction.
- Sixty days after charges have been filed, suit can be brought in a U.S. district court.
- The statute provides for jury trials.

If you're serious about taking advantage of the ADEA safety net, before you contact one of the twenty-eight regional EEOC offices, you should:

1. Look around for something you don't like (a raise that rightfully was yours, a promotion denied without merit, a derogatory remark someone made, etc.).
2. Connect it with something about yourself that relates to age or another issue such as medical condition, physical handicap, or gender.

Once you've done this, carefully and discreetly drop a word or two of bombshell legalese to your boss or other department power broker. You want to sound detached and calculating, saying little about your plans. Let management stew as it worries about an investigation, adverse publicity, and costs of mounting a defense. Just be sure to realize you're in a high-stakes game where losing could cost your job and winning is a long, difficult challenge. Here are those potent terms:

EEO Vocabulary

accessibility The provision for entry and exit of handicapped individuals at the employer's place of business.

adverse impact The rate of selection in employment decisions (transfers, promotions, relocations, etc.) that works to the disadvantage of a protected class.

affirmative action plan or program (AAP) A formal, written document enumerating the employer's policy, goals, procedures for monitoring compliance, and delegation of authority to implement equal employment opportunity laws.

aggregate workforce The entire number of employees that provides the basis for affirmative action requirements.

back pay Compensation for past economic loss (reduced wages, denied fringe benefits, etc.) that begins when a discriminatory practice occurs and ends when it is corrected.

bona fide occupational qualification (BFOQ) An official consent from a governmental compliance authority to exclude people in a protected class from performing a particular job. It is difficult to obtain and must be available for review by the aggrieved employees.

charge of discrimination (charge) The formal claim filed with the Equal Employment Opportunity Commission that begins the investigative process.

class action A civil lawsuit filed by members of a protected class alleging discrimination by the employer. It is extremely difficult to prosecute, but mentioning it tends to shake the corporate ceilings.

compliance review The official investigation that occurs as a result of a claim filed with an authorized governmental agency.

disparate effect The result of discrimination against members of a protected class. Example: not hiring a proportionate number of women to men.

EEO-1 Report An annual report filed with the Equal Employment Opportunity Commission or state regulatory agency. Separates the aggregate workforce into protected classes.

Equal Employment Opportunity Commission (EEOC) The federal compliance authority for discrimination complaints.

exemplary damages An extraordinary amount of money awarded in a civil lawsuit against the employer to set an example, thus discouraging others from perpetuating similar discrimination.

front pay Compensation for past economic loss (reduced wages, denied fringe benefits, etc.) that begins when a discriminatory practice occurs and ends when the same level of pay has been reached.

permanent injunction An order issued after the trial of a civil lawsuit requiring cessation of a discriminatory practice indefinitely.

preliminary injunction An interim order issued in a civil lawsuit requiring cessation of a discriminatory practice until the trial.

protected class (or affected class) Groups designated by age, medical condition, physical handicap, gender, race (color), religion (creed), national origin, ancestry, or arrest information. Discriminatory practices against class members by employers is unlawful.

punitive damages An extraordinary amount of money awarded in a civil lawsuit against the employer to punish him for past discrimination.

reasonable accommodation Anything necessary to alter, adjust, or modify the job, employment conditions, or place of business to overcome any objection of a protected working class member, or make it possible for an employee to overcome it on his or her own.

sexual harassment Unwelcome behavior of a sexual nature or with sexual overtones: sexual harassment takes two legal forms:

1. *Quid pro quo.* (a) Where submitting to sexual demands becomes an implicit or explicit term or condition of employment, for example, "You can have a promotion but only if you have sex with me." (b) Making decisions affecting someone's employment or compensation on the basis of whether the person submits to or rejects sexual demands.

2. *Hostile environment.* Sexual conduct that has the purpose or the effect of unreasonably interfering with a person's job performance or that creates an intimidating or offensive work environment.

support data   Statistical analysis and other documentation maintained to justify employment practices.

systemic discrimination   Continued employment policies or practices that, regardless of their intent, have the effect of perpetuating discrimination.

temporary restraining order (TRO)   An immediate order issued in a civil lawsuit that ordinarily lasts a short period of time, ordering the end to a discriminatory practice until the hearing on the preliminary injunction.

underutilization   Employment of members of a protected class at a wage rate below their availability in the labor market.

utilization analysis   A statistical procedure designed to identify underutilization.

That's the list; use it wisely and well.

Fear of Failure

You're restless and unfulfilled. Yet, now, when you should be looking for a new position with your current job still intact, you hesitate. Psychologically, you're unprepared to make the move. Although it's hard to admit, you're probably afraid of the younger competition, particularly if you're after a high visibility spot.

Dig deeper into your psyche and you'll find it's not really age that makes you resist change but the fear of failure. Now in your midthirties, you're in a comfortable, if somewhat restrictive, cocoon. Being stuck in this same spot becomes a self-fulfilling prophecy that you can't do anything else.

In *The Plateauing Trap*, Judith Bardwick writes, "Between the ages of 35 and 43, most men feel the tremendous gap between their aspirations and their attainments, between their expectations and the facts of plateauing. They must face the difference between the earlier perception that they were outstanding and the current judgment that they are of average competence."

Your Role in Overcoming Age Bias

Your role in overcoming age bias is multifaceted. There are a number of things you can do personally, professionally, and with an eye toward positioning yourself for promotion.

Personal Ways to Distance Yourself From the Age Factor

1. Work from your perspective of a more organized lifestyle.
2. Let your experience work for you. You know what works and what doesn't because you've lived it.
3. Stay current in your thinking.
4. Dress tastefully in styles that combine good taste with contemporary fashion.
5. Defuse negative thinking commentary from others. If a conversation comes up where age is mentioned, here are a few rejoinders you can tactfully use:

"Experience that comes with age really has nothing to do with this discussion."

or

"National statistics show that productivity doesn't decline with age; people age forty-five and over only had three sick days per year."

Professional Ways to Downplay the Age Factor

1. Become more valuable to your organization by making an effort to learn new skills. If you're in marketing, it's advantageous to see how the frontline troops in sales work. If you are marketing ballpoint pens, it is beneficial to learn how volume packaging achieves greater consumer visibility.
2. Learn more about a specialized area overlapping your current duties. Amy, a consultant for a trade show firm, is light years ahead of her coworkers, because her advanced computer skills also enable her to do booth layouts.
3. Take the initiative. Request a career planning and counseling meeting with your boss to find out what it takes to advance your career—more experience, better education, stronger interpersonal skills.

How to Position Yourself for Promotion With an Attitude Makeover

1. Be supportive of your boss.
2. Carefully watch and learn how others you respect motivate

employees. Whether you advance in your present job or else-where, you'll definitely need this skill.

3. Be visible. When an opportunity arises to make a presenta-tion, grab and run with it for all it's worth. Then, make sure that key players know what you're doing.

4. Show you're a team player. "Sure, I'll come in a day early to help you set up that trade show booth," or "Looks like you could use a little help with those reports. Can I assist?" Suspi-cion might be the first order of the day if you're really doing an about-face, but if you stick with the new-you attitude, it should pay off.

5. Get word out that you want a promotion. If you've been around so long that they begin to see you as part of the furni-ture, perhaps it never crossed your boss's mind that you're still in the running.

Earning (Without Demanding) Respect

Becoming professionally outdated has more to do with your personal-ity and your commitment than it does with your age. Remembering that actions speak louder than words, you're going to have to show-case your abilities to regain the status you once enjoyed. Once you've reinvented yourself you'll definitely be worth a lot more!

1. *Identify seminars that can benefit your company and offer to attend.* When you return, write a comprehensive memo about how your firm can implement new strategies, and make sure it gets circulated in all the right places.

2. *Be the authoritative information source.* Let people know that you know how to get more information as problems arise. Then read, clip, and distribute what you've learned. Being wise doesn't help if no one knows you know.

3. *Request new books and trade journals relative to your department's responsibilities.* Then be prepared to quote the experts in meetings. The new you looks mighty impressive when the authorities back you up.

4. *Initiate requests to study or experiment with innovative ideas, and work on them after hours.* Word will get around.

5. *Offer to become a mentor for younger employees.* The halo effect can work in reverse and shine back on you.

6. *Enjoy the benefits of your hard-earned experience.* While younger employees worry about new assignments or giving oral presentations, you can achieve more with less effort based on those years in the trenches.

Chapter 4

Breaking Through the Ten-Year Career Barrier

If you learn nothing else from this book, there's one thing you should emblazon on your mind: Business is common sense and business understanding is highly transferable. Since that's the case, experience is your primary asset.

Even in the most technical fields like law and medicine, only 10 percent of the time is spent using specialized skills. The other 90 percent is (hopefully) common sense and good judgment. In many industries, employers actually prefer to bring in crossover talent with new ideas rather than people with years in the same business whose vision may be narrower. Armed with your background skills and experience, you can broaden your perspective across a much wider range of job possibilities.

How to Broaden Your Career Horizons in a Hurry

As an employment counselor, I've used the following technique with great success (see Exhibit 4-1). Take a blank sheet of ruled paper and draw a vertical line down the middle. Label the left-hand side Job Family Skills. Label the right-hand side Crossover Jobs.

In the left-hand column list all the skills related to your present job. Let's say you're an advertising copywriter. As a physical skill, you know computer word processing. Through experience, your professional skills include the ability to take a new product and define a marketing platform based on its benefits. In in-house meetings you are able to verbalize these concepts. As a writer, you can set them down based on the layouts worked out with the art director and account executive. Now, where can you plug in these skills to expand

Exhibit 4-1. Matching current skills with future jobs for advertising copywriter.

Job Family Skills	Crossover Jobs
Word processing	Secretary? No.
Ability to define marketing platform for a new product	Account executive?
Can verbalize marketing concepts at meetings	Ad manager for major client?
Write around layouts	Writer in public relations? TV newswriting?
Liaise with art director and account executive	Account executive? Art director? Probably not.
_____	_____
_____	_____

beyond the limited advertising agency world? Once you've begun working through them, your mind will come up with all sorts of creative options. Write them down, no matter how trivial they appear at first.

Now, move on to the right-hand column. Obviously with your word processing background you could be a secretary, but that's hardly the job jump you had in mind. Reviewing your professional skills gets you thinking across such fields as ad manager for a major client, a writer in public relations, or even a move into TV newswriting.

Once you go through the obvious, you can find many more crossover jobs by reading the *Directory of Occupational Titles,* published annually by the U.S. Department of Labor. It contains the names and brief descriptions of thousands of jobs and is available at your public library reference desk.

There is a major difference between skills that are actually transferable, like the word processing example above, and those that can be marketed as transferable. Once you've looked at half a dozen job descriptions you find appealing, take each job description and write down the skills in the Job Family Skills list and see how well they plug into your newly expanded list of professional possibilities. You probably didn't realize you had all that talent and expertise applicable to so many fields!

Become a Skill Merchant

In the September 1993 issue of *Working Woman,* Stephen M. Pollan and Mark Levine succinctly defined the new workplace where corporate paternalism and its security blanket has been yanked off, and "You'll be like a free agent in professional sports. . . . In the age of corporate loyalty, you were your job. In the age of the skill merchant, when every job amounts to a temporary project, such close identification is unhealthy for your psyche and unproductive for your career."

In the same article, Susan Garbrecht, senior vice president and director of human resources at Sotheby's, advises, "Identify yourself as a package of skills rather than as a job description."

Among the skills that are most important in today's job market are:

1. Managing and reviewing the activities of others
2. Motivating through leadership roles or sales presentations
3. Researching and analyzing technical data
4. Creating and developing services or products
5. Fabricating and manufacturing items for commercial or private consumption

In addition, the future will see the need for computer literacy, written communication, public and presentational speaking, and foreign language communications.

Armed with your own list of skills, you need to start talking with people in the range of fields you've defined to see what opportunities exist. (Chapter 5 tells you how and just what to say.) Remember, almost all your managerial skills are transferable to other businesses and industries. You should also be aware of those you could qualify for with slight additional training. If you've only worked in private industry, you may find challenging opportunities with nonprofit agencies or in the public sector.

Sam Thompson made a quick rise to assistant vice president of purchasing at a top U.S. airline. Then the bottom dropped out of the airline markets. Groomed as a "comer" for years, Sam got his first negative annual review. Although it was never admitted, Sam realized he was being forced out because of his high salary. When he finally left, he moved his valuable purchasing and management skills over to the county he lived in, as director of purchasing. It didn't matter that he was now buying trash trucks instead of flight simulators—the bidding processes were the same.

The bottom line is that experience is not what you've done but what you do with what you've done. The key is to translate your basic job experience into specifically marketable attributes. I call it your experience inventory.

Developing Your Experience Inventory

Take a good long look at your job history. Here's how: Start with your employment history and write down every job you've ever held. Yes, go back all the way to that newspaper route or sales job at the local fast-food chain. Use a form such as the one shown in Exhibit 4-2.

Based on that complete listing, then break out the information on an individual job summary form, such as the one shown in Exhibit 4-3. Feel free to copy it and use one page per job.

Don't bother with specific duties or how much you earned. Just inventory all experience—responsibilities and results. Especially results. They are what really matter. On the dynamic resume you're going to write, you'll look so good you'll hardly recognize yourself. Yet, it will all be true—just don't skimp on the details now.

Each experience affects your present attitudes, goals, and marketability. Most people don't realize how similar jobs are, all the way from director of administration to PTA president. Going back to your first job (mine was as a holiday employee at the post office, where I had to learn the mail scheme), each job teaches one or more skills that can be used in future jobs. My first job taught me an eye for remembering details that I've been using all my working life.

Next, review your achievements. Early accomplishments may seem inconsequential, but they help establish attributes you may have forgotten. Go through old records. Get down those dusty high school and college annuals and make yourself remember your achievements as editor of the school paper or president of your fraternity. Once you've assembled all this information, you're ready to convert it to a usable form. Begin by asking yourself some very important questions.

- What are your primary attributes?
- What are your primary liabilities?
- Which jobs did you like most?
- Which achievements give you the greatest sense of pride?
- Do you prefer working in small or large organizations?
- Do you like the security of having a job or do you prefer being your own boss?

Exhibit 4-2.   Job inventory.

Dates		Job Title	Name of Company
To:	From:		

- Do you prefer supervisory responsibilities or would you rather do the work yourself?
- Do you prefer working with people or with things?
- Is a salary mandatory or do you want to test your potential earning capabilities with a commission/bonus system?
- Do you like to travel?

Now, prepare another sheet for each job, using Exhibit 4-3 as a guide. Give it an identifying job number. With the information you've answered about yourself, use it to outline your ideal job. Be realistic.

Exhibit 4-3. Individual job summary form.

Job No.

Date: From _____, 19___ to _____, 19___

Company name: _____

Address: _____

_____

Telephone: _____

Reported to: _____

Potential references still employed there: _____

_____

Significant responsibilities: _____

_____

_____

_____

_____

_____

_____

_____

Significant results (in descending order of importance):

1. _____

2. _____

3. _____

4. _____

5. _____

State what you really want and list your liabilities. In this way, you have the clearest picture of where you want to go and the place you'd like to work.

Doing these exercises may be time consuming, but they pay off. What you'll wind up with is the format to help you break out of your career slump.

Widening the Scope and Looking Up

By now, you should have an accurate and detailed picture of your experience. You should also have a vision of your ideal workplace. You might not get all you want with a change of scene, but knowing the route can make it a whole lot easier to move up your chosen career path.

What's next? Figuring out if you're really ready to make a major career move. Write down the following twelve questions and give yourself time to answer them. Your answers will show you whether it's time to move or stay put.

1. Are you satisfied or unsatisfied with the work itself in your current position?
2. Do you enjoy your worksite, or is the environment unsatisfactory?
3. Do you require more challenge?
4. Ideally, what form would this challenge take?
5. If you're being sufficiently challenged, are you being fairly compensated?
6. Are you upper management material? Could you be an effective facilitator?
7. Do you have a time frame for making a career move?
8. What are the major factors that figure into such a time frame (a) at work, (b) at home, (c) other?
9. What might happen if you do not make a change?
10. Can you live with the status quo?
11. If not, how much effort are you willing to expend to make a change?
12. Do you need new skills for the job change you are envisioning?

Since most people don't live in a vacuum, ask your family and/or close friends what they think you would enjoy doing and what might bring you greater work satisfaction. Their answers may give you some eye-opening viewpoints and may clarify your final decision.

How to Prepare for the Search

With your mind made up to move, it's time to get organized. To begin, you need a written or computer-based filing system with the following categories:

- *Close contacts.* Friends and people in your own company you genuinely trust.
- *Extended contacts.* This group comprises your basic networking group. Who is included depends on how discreet you judge that person to be. However, it usually includes long-standing personal and professional acquaintances. One of your primary advantages ten years into your career and what puts you ahead of younger job seekers are these contacts. Since you already know people in your industry and community and have acquired a larger range of acquaintances than the newcomers, you're in a better position to begin tapping these resources.
- *The widest possible networking contacts.* These might be family members, acquaintances current and former even if you have to make a phone call to get them to recall you, employers, coworkers, supervisors, subordinates, professional colleagues, clients and customers of current and former employers, vendors and suppliers, even friendly competitors, members of every business, fraternal, or social organization you belong to, church members, and neighbors. If there's a special professor from a university where you've taken an advanced degree or even one who might recall you favorably from your undergrad days, jot the name down. You may not necessarily contact them immediately or may not use them at all, but the list is ready when you need it.

Then:

- *Start getting your references in order.* I'll go into greater detail in Chapter 10, but for now let your mind wander freely and compile as broad a list as possible, divided into personal and professional reference categories.
- *Update your professional telephone directory.* Include specific new

job lead contacts. Even the most tangential tip is worth noting for future follow-up.

▪ *Review trade journals.* Clip important news with names of people you might want to contact or companies whose future plans may include you—even if they don't know it yet! Some of the best sources for identifying trade magazine listings for your industry include *Bacon's Publicity Checker, Gale Directory of Publications, Business Periodicals Index, Job Hunter's Sourcebook: Where to Find Employment Leads and Other Job Search Resources,* and the *Encyclopedia of Business Information Sources.* Most should be available in major libraries.

▪ *List upcoming professional meetings.* If your current job permits you to attend meetings or seminars, it's an excellent source of additional contacts. Just don't tip your hand to your plans at this point.

▪ *Begin reviewing lists of headhunters and employment agencies* (more about this in Chapter 12). Today's computerized placement networks give agencies the ability to access thousands of job openings and mesh them with backgrounds of applicants in a single zip code or anywhere else. Since you're already employed, be discreet and follow these guidelines:

1. Only one counselor per agency may call you at the office.
2. Everything related to your search much be mailed to your home.
3. Discretion must be used by the agency to protect your current job.

▪ *Update your resume(s).* Yes, you may need more than one, depending on the variety of positions you'll be applying for.

▪ *Develop a list of potential contact companies.* These should include:

1. The ideal companies you've read about.
2. Companies profiled in business/employment publications such as the *Wall Street Journal's National Employment Weekly.*
3. Companies listed in local chamber of commerce directories. Many such guides include descriptions of the companies and the names of their human resources directors. (Resist the urge to call these people. For now, all you want is information.) I'll show you a far better way to direct your search to the right decision maker in Chapter 5.
4. Organizations frequently mentioned in trade journals.
5. Referrals from personal contacts.
6. The competition in your industry.

7. Companies suggested by your alumni association and professional groups.

The Hottest Second Decade Jobs

Now that you've created your basic list, here's a yardstick to measure what the experts see as most promising fields for your career's crucial second decade. (Of course all the prognosticating in the world won't get you that single perfect spot. But the trend indicators can point you in the right direction.) *Fortune* magazine reports by the middle of the 1990s through 1996 that midsize companies that employ between one hundred and one thousand people will fuel the hottest job growth. "Representing a mere 4 percent of all companies nationally, these midsize businesses are expected to create 33 percent of all jobs over the next two years, perhaps 33 million in all," says *Fortune.*

Although the number of managers needed will continue to shrink and it will continue to become more difficult to rise through traditional ranks, there are opportunities aplenty in the next ten years if you know where to look. In July 1993, the U.S. Bureau of Labor Statistics broke out projected job growth between 1990 and 2005. The hottest opportunities?

▪ *Computer professionals.* The greatest need will be for information service specialists. "Today the guys who are successful are the guys who have control of information. It used to be the jocks had the power. They're not important anymore. The guys born to master information are the new ruling elite," exults one software designer in a November 1993 *Los Angeles Times* story on the "Revenge of the Nerds."

Jobs for computer systems analysts and scientists will increase nearly 80 percent to 829,000. Programmers will jump by more than 50 percent to over 880,000. Electrical engineers who specialize in telecommunications will have a 22 percent growth rate by 2003 according to the Bureau of Labor Statistics (BLS). These jobs will be necessary to keep up with the information explosion as the economy continues to convert from military to consumer and industrial production for civilian use. Instead of being on the sidelines managing company data, these information specialists will move into frontline management in charge of networking.

Just down the employment ladder from management positions will be the cadre of support personnel including 1.2 million new jobs for drafters who work with computer-assisted systems.

▪ *Health care specialists.* Spurred by the health reforms of the mid 1990s, health care careers will grow much faster than in the '80s, with the exception of dentistry. Although nurses will be in the vanguard with over 35 percent more positions projected, the need for physicians will increase from 25 percent to 34 percent, with the dental ranks growing only from between 5 to 13 percent.

According to many surveys, these special health care fields are also worth noting:

1. Physical therapists with a growth rate predicted to be 76 percent by the year 2005.
2. Physician assistants who are qualified to do up to 80 percent of the tasks done by a physician and whose demand is increasing because of the increased need for such skills in nursing homes and HMOs. A 34 percent increase is expected by 2005.
3. Radiologic technicians are now in such great demand that for every 4,500 graduates there are 6,000 potential employment openings. The BLS predicts a 69.5 percent increase in need by 2005.
4. Nurse anesthetists, known as Certified Registered Nurse Anesthetists (CRNAs), are in a burgeoning profession with 35,400 needed by 2010. To meet that need, the number of students currently graduating each year must triple! Particularly hot: specialists in open heart surgery and obstetrics.
5. Home health services managers will be in heavy demand. By 2005 the number of home health care specialists is expected to double, fueling the need for managers to determine home health care options.
6. Environmental engineering, a field that is related to public well-being, is one of the largest projected growth areas. The Department of Energy alone has $38 billion budgeted from 1993 to 1997 to clean up waste sites. Private companies are desperate for individuals who can figure out the Environmental Protection Agency's stringent new regulations. Currently only one-third of the required number of professionals are being trained.
7. Architects specializing in health care design are in top demand. Latest statistics show $12.4 billion spent on health-related construction in 1991. Factoring in the aging populace, the emphasis on health care reform, and the Americans With Disabilities Act accentuates requirements for architects who specialize in designing for the needs of the disabled and ill.

▪ *Marketing specialists.* Segueing from health care into marketing, one of the best fields will be biotechnology sales. More new products were approved in 1991 than in the entire history of the industry. But there is a gaping hole in the number of sales professionals who can knowledgeably speak about DNA, monoclonal antibodies, and enzymes that target diseases more efficiently than synthetic drugs. Major marketing opportunities will also exist for:

1. Mature market consultants. By the year 2000, around one-third of the population will be over age fifty, and even now that group represents 40 percent of consumer demand. People with an eye for the tastes of this burgeoning market are needed to become the consultants, account executives, and product managers for this market segment.
2. Home entertainment market specialists. Those knowledgeable about the whims of Americans who now spend $7.8 billion on movie rentals for the 83 percent of current homes with VCRs are going to be widely courted in the twenty-first century. Employers will include studios, independent production companies, and cable networks.

▪ *Management.* Several hot fields expected to experience at least a 35 percent growth rate by 2005 include marketing, advertising, and public relations managers. Just behind, with a projected growth of from 25 percent to 34 percent are property and real estate managers, loan officers and counselors, and construction contractors and managers.

▪ *Financial services.* Between widely fluctuating interest rates and the labyrinth of new tax laws, qualified certified financial planners will be greatly in demand. U.S. accounting firms are setting up shop overseas in a big way. Accountants who specialize in tax, management consulting, and auditing are needed at home and overseas to analyze tax liabilities and comply with foreign tax structures. Demand has increased 200 percent since 1990, with no signs of letting up. In banking, as the 1980s financial debacle ebbs, there is still need for individuals who can restructure loans and turn poor or nonperforming assets into better performers. These loan workout specialists typically have backgrounds in finance, banking, and investment, usually with loan review or auditing experience. Actuaries who assess the risk of sickness or accidents that may result in claims to insurance companies are in short supply. No wonder—it takes twenty-three exams to become certified, and usually half fail the first round!

▪ *The legal profession.* With the economy in the doldrums and projections unpromising, bankrupcy attorneys continue in demand. Employment attorneys are also in a strong growth position. Too bad I'm not at the start of my career!

Chapter 5

How to Track the Best Hidden Jobs

If it's been a while since your last venture into the job market, things have changed. The best jobs are nowhere to be seen in public print. So what to do? Use the research media of choice—the Yellow Pages. They outperform all other sources for tracking down hidden jobs. Another excellent source is the industry directories in your public libraries. And straight ahead on the electronic superhighway are myriad ways to go on-line with your job search.

These jobs don't come conveniently advertised in the classified section of your newspaper. You have to make calls to get the information. That's the downside. (Chapter 7 tells how to call and exactly what to say.) The upside is often, "First come, first served." You get to the elusive prize without standing in a long line of job seekers.

The Yellow Pages

For years, the Yellow Pages have run variations of one particularly memorable TV commercial. Its theme: "If you can't find it in here, it probably doesn't exist." When you let your mind roam free in its search for job categories to market your own package of transferable job skills, the Yellow Pages can be its most valuable ally.

Unless you're in retail or a field that is visible to consumers, the local Business-to-Business Yellow Pages will be an invaluable research aid. Look up the categories that interest you. In turn, these will likely be cross-referenced to related fields. What will you find? Information ranges from company names and phone numbers (basic listings) to full page ads with substantive vital data including product lines, headquarters, and branch locations. Because they are updated more frequently than others, the business-to-business directories often have listings of up-and-coming companies as well as major players. With midsize companies creating approximately a third of all jobs within the next two years, targeting midrange and smaller firms for a large portion of your search makes especially good sense.

Get information for distant cities from the library or nearest major airport. Or purchase a telephone directory for any U.S. city through Pacific Bell at (800) 848-8000.

Take the information on each company that appeals to you and file it with your list of potential companies to contact. The best method is to use a single sheet of yellow lined paper or a five-by-eight-inch index card for each company you are considering. Then alphabetize. Leave plenty of space for taking notes. You can create similar forms on your computer word processing or database program.

In case you doubt the success of the Yellow Pages as a search tool, here's proof from my own experience. Often I've been in cities on book tours at radio or TV shows where I've been asked to place the most impossibly disadvantaged person who has virtually no marketable skills. Offstage I do a miniinterview of the job seeker, hole up with my trusty Yellow Pages, and by show's end, I've arranged two to three interviews for this unlikely candidate. Then I'm back on the air looking like a hero. Believe me, it works!

Industry Directories

Your goal is to identify and build personalized background information on companies within your designated geographic area. Block out one full day to go to the nearest major library. Usually, they're open on Saturdays and some of the main branches of city libraries may even have Sunday hours.

Check with the reference librarian for these valuable search tools:

- Annual Reports (publicly held corporations)
- *Business Periodicals Index* (H.W. Wilson Company)
- *Dun & Bradstreet's Million Dollar Directory*
- *Moody's New Reports*
- *Moody's Manuals*
- *Standard and Poor's Register of Corporations, Directors and Executives* (particularly useful for senior candidates)
- *Standard and Poor's Corporation Records*
- *Thomas Register of American Manufacturers*
- *MacRae's Blue Book*
- *Value Line Investment Surveys*

Others that can prove valuable in specific areas include:

- The *Almanac of American Employers Corporate Jobs Outlook*
- *Corporate Technology Directory*
- *Directory of Corporate Affiliations*
- *Directory of Leading Private Companies*
- *Encyclopedia of Associations*
- *The JobBank Guide to Employment Services*
- *The JobBank Series*
- *The National JobBank*
- *Sales Guides to High-Tech Companies*

There are also additional books targeting specific fields such as medicine, law, government, and engineering.

You'll quickly be up to your eyeballs in reference works. Scan first to see which ones you'll spend your valuable time on. Then develop a page per potential employer with the following information:

- Name and address
- Phone (main)
- Phone (human resources)
- Name of human resources director
- Name of president
- Name of chief operating officer
- Director related to your job specialty (i.e., marketing, sales, finance)
- List of products
- Specific products or services in the geographic region you're targeting
- Yearly sales in dollars
- Profits
- Recent acquisitions and/or divestitures

On-Line Data Sources

Computer databases have speeded up everything related to information management. Their biggest advantage is availability, with information that even the largest libraries may not have. There are several ways to access this information. CompuServe is the least expensive and most easily accessible through your home computer modem, although others may be on-line by the time you read this. On-line data sources at your local public library may include GEnie, DIALOG, BRS, ORBIT, NEXIS, Dow Jones News/Retrieval, and NewsNet.

Some database companies will do the grunt work of generating leads for you, based on any relevant parameters you choose, such as all the midsize gaming industry manufacturers in the state of Nevada. Beware. Such services can get expensive. But if money's no object and time is crucial you can call: Seagate & Associates (201) 262-5200 or (800) 992-5520, Dun & Bradstreet Information Services (201) 605-6000 or (800) 634-5669, or Finders/The Advantage (301) 788-0500 or (800) 628-9685. For others, check your library for *The Fiscal Directory of Fee Based Information Services in Libraries,* published by FYI, a department of the County of Los Angeles Public Library at (310) 868-4003 or (800) 582-1093.

Information Interviewing: Fastest, Most Accurate Market Research

At this point, all your basic information should be in place. Now you're ready to refine it by calling for updates. Even with the latest on-line research, information quickly becomes dated and useless. If the marketing director has just been replaced, and he was your target for an interview, you'd better know about the personnel change.

To get the most from your phone conversation, plan a brief script of what you'll ask. You're not yet calling for an interview. You're determining whether a company is worth any further investment of your time and effort.

Based on what you already know about the target, prepare a worksheet with as many of these questions as need updating. Leave plenty of space for the answers. When you call, be quick and to the point.

- Who is in charge of department X?
- What products does the company make or what services does it offer? (It's essential that you know this by the time you are interviewed, so that you can ask relevant questions.)
- What are its major markets? (During the interview, you'll want to throw in informational tidbits showing you understand what the company is doing.)
- Is it publicly held or privately owned?
- Is it a nonprofit organization or governmental agency?
- How many employees does it have? 10 or fewer? 11 to 50? 50 to

100? 100 to 999? over 1,000? The answer may help you see how you'll feel in a larger or smaller firm.

- Does the employer have new products? (Suggests growth potential and opportunity.)
- What is the precise nature of the duties and skills involved in the position? (You may not be able to get this information if they're playing close to the vest, but Chapter 6 tells you how to break through the stone wall.)
- Is the employer gaining in market share? Is the industry on an up climb or a downward spiral? (Don't necessarily write off companies in jeopardy. If it's a smaller firm and you have something real to offer the owner, you could be in an excellent negotiating posture. Ronald Sears, a computer technician with management aspirations, talked with the owner of a stumbling, financially strapped materials handling manufacturer. When invited in for a healthy salary, Sears's fresh viewpoint helped get creditors off the president's back to give the company some needed breathing space.)
- What is the financial outlook of the company? Are mergers or restructurings impending? Are layoffs expected? (Again, this situation might not be bad. For example, if you're seeking a position in the volatile airlines industry with its multiyear record of red ink, you could be much in demand at senior levels if your background is strong in union negotiations.)

Whom Should I Call?

If you're phoning a large publicly held corporation, call the investor relations or corporate communications department and ask for their literature. If you use these two sources expect to receive positive outlook, slick publications. Be wary if you call the public relations department; these departments are often staffed by no-nonsense former business journalists, so you might get some pop questions asked like "Who are you?" and "What do you know about us?"

Your first line of information for smaller companies is the local Better Business Bureau. You can learn the owner's name, number of years in business, even if there are any consumer complaints outstanding. Since the information providers have no personal ax to grind or are not trying to shield the boss from you, ask away. Another option is to call sales, marketing, or even the receptionist and state the purpose of your call. Plan on doing a lot of listening, with paper and pen handy.

Assuming you haven't reached someone on deadline, you'll find that people love to talk about their jobs and companies. There may even be a bonus in the conversation in the form of an internal referral if a position is opening up. If Ann Smith in sales suggests you speak with John Jenkins in marketing, Jenkins will probably want to see the candidates that Smith already feels good about. Of course, you'll have to ask for the referral, but wait until the end of the conversation before crossing that bridge.

Other good sources of information for smaller firms include vendors, customers, or previous employees.

Efficient Personal Telephone Interviewing

By your research, you've now established that Consolidated Bakeries is a prime job target. Who do you talk to? Depending on what you need to know, you start at the very bottom or very top of the pyramid. Do not, under any circumstances, make a call for an interview until you know the best person to field your request.

When you don't know the name of that individual, ask the switchboard operator or receptionist the name of the person in charge of your target department.

Say something like, "I'm writing a letter to supermarket sales and want to get the department manager's name." If that doesn't work, try using a fictitious name in the department. "Is Phil Zeiler still in charge of supermarket sales?" Obviously, the telephone voice on the other end won't know the name you've given, but will probably respond with "No, the person you want is Ellen Lansing."

Be sure to verify spelling, title, address including suite or floor number, and the correct phone extension.

At this point you may have the overwhelming urge to be put through to your prospect. Don't do it until you've read Chapter 7.

When you think you know the target prospect's name but aren't positive, verify it. Ask the operator or receptionist, "Is Richard Fleming still vice president of plant operations. And does he prefer to be called Richard, Rich, or Rick?"

Your primary goal is to build on a warm and friendly environment, which is not easy when you're essentially making a cold call. Even the most rank amateur can sense the go/no go signals emanating from the other end of the line. If you get an "I'm busy, let's get this over with" feeling, don't pursue further questions. But if warm fuzzies are conjured up in the operator's tone, you can push for more details like: "Does he come into work early or stay late? I'm planning to meet with him. Do you know if he'll be around next week? What's a good time to reach him?"

Also be sure to get the name of the gatekeeper to your employment target. Usually, it's his or her secretary or assistant. Then when you make your interview call, you can sound friendlier by saying, "Shirley, this is David Alcala calling to speak with Mr. Fleming." Just that one name makes the call warmer.

Sometimes it pays to start at the top of the company and work your way downward. Let's say you know the president is Stephen McHugh. Call the receptionist and ask for his secretary's name. Then ask to be put through. When Lucy Secretary comes on the line, your dialogue might sound like this:

> "Lucy, this is Susan Sherman. I wanted to find out who's in charge of advertising, but the receptionist put me through to you. I'm sorry to trouble you but I would like to know who heads up advertising."

Then recheck, "How do you spell that?" and finish by asking, "Can you put me through or should I go back to the switchboard?" If you don't get the answer you need from one secretary, try the next down the line. Then, when you finally get to the correct department, you can truthfully say that "Lucy in Mr. McHugh's office suggested that I speak with Mr. Atkins in advertising."

With this technique you almost always get through to a decision maker. Often you get added cooperation through a preliminary conversation with his or her secretary.

With the latest information and correct contact names of at least a dozen likely prospects, begin to prioritize the order of your calls.

Is There Any Future for You in the Help Wanteds?

As part of a well-rounded job search you should review the print media. Where the ads are, though, are not necessarily where the jobs are. Only 15 percent of available jobs are advertised; I recommend you spend not more than 25 percent of your time on this source. Where *should* you look?

• The Sunday newspaper is the spot to look for professional positions. In addition to the classifieds, often the major city papers will list ads in the business section, under a catch-all title such as Career Opportunities. These are generally larger display ads that spell out specific job responsibilities and requirements. They give you far greater opportunity to learn more about a position than the two-or-three liners in the classifieds.

- Tuesday's *Wall Street Journal* usually carries new ads.

- *WSJ*'s *National Business Employment Weekly* combines ads from all four regions of the journal and covers listings for a week. To subscribe, call 1-800-JOB-HUNT.

- The *National Ad Search*. It lists ads from seventy-five major newspapers. To subscribe call 1-800-922-2832.

- Computer bulletin boards are the latest in expanding job search options.

- Desirable ads sometime appear in some not-so-obvious spots:

1. The career planning center of your alma mater.
2. Small local daily newspapers or even weeklies. Companies may recruit in specific areas to reduce the number of applicants and find individuals who will not have to commute long distances.
3. Specialized technical publications and newsletters. Check the following at your library: *Where the Jobs Are: A Comprehensive Directory of 1200 Career Opportunities* or *Job Hunters Sourcebook: Where to Find Employment Leads and Other Job Search Resources*.

- *Commerce Business Daily* lists U.S. government procurement invitations, contract awards, subcontracting leads, sales of surplus property, and foreign trade opportunities. By reading the Contract Awards section, for example, you can identify companies that have won government contracts. From this general source can come a gold mine of possibilities, to be followed up with a phone call to your professional counterpart in the listed organization. Based on his or her response, you can follow up with your resume. To order *Commerce Business Daily*, call (203) 783-3238 with your Visa or MasterCard.

Responding to Open Ads

Remember: Send only resumes to human resources departments, no cover letters. If the ad has a department number, call and try to connect to a specific person. Then and only then enclose a dynamic cover letter to that person that matches your skills to the job's requirements. A graphic way is to use a format that lists the ad's requirements on the left side of the page and your matching skills on the right (see Exhibit 5-1). If they don't match exactly, make sure the skills you list exceed the qualifications required. Another option is the standard paragraph format (see Exhibit 5-2).

Exhibit 5-1.   Chart format: Letter resume to a want ad.

6384 Leffingwell Road
Los Angeles, CA 90064
(555) 873-5402

August 2, 1995

Henry Porter
Professional Employment Department
Grant Hotel
341 N. Hill Street
Los Angeles, CA 90005

Dear Mr. Porter:

In response to your ad in the most recent Sunday edition of the *Los Angeles Times* for a director of housekeeping, I feel my qualifications favorably match your requirements.

YOUR REQUIREMENTS	MY QUALIFICATIONS
• Solid experience in property and plant maintenance	15+ years experience plant maintenance management including:
• Minimum five years housekeeping	7 years housekeeping supervision
• Optional grounds management background	Grounds management experience Custodial operations Security systems Fire prevention

Enclosed please find my resume for your confidential review. Salary history may be discussed during an interview. I look forward to meeting with you in the near future.

Sincerely yours,

Stewart Enders
Enclosure

Exhibit 5-2.   Paragraph response to want ad letter.

5373 Walnut Grove Street
Boston, MA 02914
(617) 555-1894

March 23, 1995

Helen Groves
Human Resources Department
ELENDER RESOURCES, INC.
3122 Beechnut Lane
Boston, MA 02963

Dear Ms. Groves:

I type 120 wpm. I'm accurate. I'm proficient in WordPerfect 6.0 (both DOS and Windows), and I work well under pressure, with minimum supervision. Your ad in today's *Boston Globe* for a word processing specialist lists those skills and qualities as being desirable.

I have ten years of experience as a word processor. My last two employers also were in the computer field. They faced numerous deadlines that required dependable word processing capabilities. I've never missed a deadline and I willingly work overtime to get the job done.

I would appreciate an opportunity to interview for this position and to demonstrate my word processing skills. I will call you on Friday to see when we might schedule such a meeting

Sincerely,

Ellen Chase
Enclosure

To get the most *bang* from your letter, particularly if it's a company you really want to work for, don't just limit your letter and resume to the department stated in the ad. Call and identify other related departments and contact them as well.

Seeing Through the Want Ads

If you're determined to answer the want ads, knowing how to read them can save you time and grief.

Regardless of how they read, there are only four types of open ads:

1. *Gobbledygook* (25 percent). These ads just don't mean what they say or say what they mean. A telephone call is particularly helpful in these cases because the interviewer may not have determined what she's looking for. With artful pacing, you can appear to be what the interviewer sees in her mind's eye. An immediate interview is imperative so that you become the personification of the desired applicant.

2. *Completely misleading* (35 percent). Often these ads are for "glamour" industries like advertising or entertainment. Or they may have inflated titles for high-level management or senior marketing positions. Often these are bait and switch ads—intentionally misleading to get you into another position or identify you as someone on a job hunt. Inadvertently misleading ads contain ambiguities that were not immediately obvious to the interviewer when the ad was placed. Either way, your chances are slim. It's not worth spending much time working this kind of ad.

3. *Information missing* (25 percent). These ads omit essential duties but are long on buzzwords. Reading between the lines helps a lot here. You stand an excellent chance of passing the initial interview by studying the advertisement carefully and using it as your theme. After all, you need to know only slightly more than the interviewer about the technical part of the job.

4. *Honest and sincere* (15 percent). They list job duties, responsibilities, and minimum hiring requirements. Unfortunately for you, they've probably been broadcast far and wide through other channels and posted on employee bulletin boards. Your chances of getting hired probably depend on rigorous, objective criteria, but understanding the ad thoroughly and emphasizing your corresponding attributes will improve them. These are the employers worth pursuing. They know what they are looking for.

Responding to Blind Ads—The Great Unknown

My rule of thumb for answering blind ads is very simple—don't, if you have even the slightest intuition that it may be your company. With your neck on the line, you'd better read long and hard and in between the lines. Really desirable-sounding jobs with blind box numbers often bring in hundreds of responses, so if the job description truly sounds like it was written with you in mind, here's one ploy to enhance your chances of getting an answer. Often a lower-level human resources department prescreens the responses that come in during the week following the ad. It's worth sending a copy of the original letter and resume with a cover note about two weeks later. That way, your resume may be reviewed twice, once after the company has a better idea of the available candidate pool.

In short, blind box ads should be your last resort.

Chapter 6

Your Unique Resume Kit

For an employer, the resume is a screening device that enables the busy interviewer to eliminate candidates as quickly and painlessly as possible. For you, a resume should be a seamlessly crafted, tightly edited sales promotion piece. How can you reconcile these two seemingly divergent positions? By ensuring that your resume is tailored to generate the interview. You do this by distilling your experience to the purest, most meaningful specifics and achievements.

What format to use? The chronological and its first cousin the linear are most favored for traditional occupations where logical job progression is paramount. Targeted resumes work best when you have a very specific job in mind. Functional can be useful when you are changing careers. It also may work when you have some problems in your past—too many jobs or unexplained gaps between positions.

Many large companies now have computerized databases for electronic resumes. These resumes are a variation of the standard chronological or linear format with one major exception: At the top, in place of a standard summary, you list a series of keyword nouns that name your skills, talents, experience, and abilities.

If you've spent the time on the personal inventories in Chapter 4, you're well prepared to begin writing. Even if the prospect of yet another writing exercise makes you gag, resist the temptation to turn and go to a commercial resume agency.

There are two very important reasons for writing your own resume:

1. The mental stimulation will translate to better interviews as you relearn and reorganize your own best selling points.
2. Resume writers make everyone sound alike, and interviewers can easily spot them. Some resume services even send out their identical sounding resumes to the same core list of potential employers!

When you're done, your resume should reveal one concise, carefully worded, grammatically correct, properly spelled portrait suitable for framing. Fight your own way through it. And make every word count.

Important Know-Hows and Know-Whos

Senior executives, middle managers, and professionals like you already have carried significant responsibilities. You can expect to be held to more rigorous standards in resume portrayal than a junior executive or newly arrived college graduate. What follows are proven strategies to consider before you begin writing. Set your goal and organize to achieve it. Your resume should reflect your ability to define an objective, develop the appropriate strategy—and succeed! Strategic considerations for changing jobs include:

- Name of desired position
- Its responsibilities and potential
- Type of industry and company
- Company size
- Who you will report to
- What you will report
- Anticipated salary
- Preferred geographic location
- Type of office environment

Write all this down. Then distill it into one or two concise statements. This is just for you, private and confidential. Your resume won't state an objective, but virtually everything on it will point to your goal.

Now memorize it and say it like a mantra. Drive it into your subconscious. Making your own dream job happen begins with clearly formulating it. Once you target positions that meet your objectives, your resume is more likely to meet employer needs.

Analyze what the employer wants. You must sell the features (qualifications) and benefits (performance) of the product (you) and services (yours). Answer the questions that point to a problem-solving solution leading to a company's stronger bottom line. Intrinsically, your resume should answer these questions:

- How can I increase a company's productivity?
- How can I improve its profits and services?

- What results demonstrate my ability to perform?
- What is my knowledge of a prospective employer's business?
- How can I help make the hirer look wise in selecting me?

Know who will be reviewing your resume. Career strategy books often advise you to contact top-level officers when you seek a senior position. Addressing your resume to the CEO, CFO, COO, or senior vice president is fine. It will get you in the right bailiwick. But don't expect these individuals to read it. That task will likely fall to a director or manager, usually in human resources. Why is this important? Because when recommending a candidate back to his superior, the manager or director has a vested interest in making sure the person meets essential requirements. If you pass this screening, you're in good shape.

Don't go way back in writing your resume. Hit hard on your most applicable, current, impressive achievements.

Mention outside activities only if they help. A good example demonstrates value to the company and skills you will use in your work, for example, management and leadership of a successful community fund-raising campaign. Avoid anything that might possibly tie in race or religion. It's illegal to discriminate for these reasons, but why take a chance? If you were in the military as an officer, include your accomplishments. If you enlisted or were a noncommissioned officer, use this information only to explain a gap in employment.

Mention unusual experiences only if they drive up your value. Self-employment or time off for "self-discovery" can work for or against you. A year-long trip around the world is not beneficial, but two years in the Peace Corps would be. So would a year-long executive management program at a business school.

If you were self-employed but decided to return to other employment, in a cover letter you can explain that the company made you an offer "too good to refuse."

Keep your resume short. One page is best. At this point, you're probably saying, "I've got so much to tell." But it probably won't be read. If you're an engineer or scientist with extensive academic and professional credentials or a top-level executive you may go to two pages. Shorter is better 99 percent of the time.

What NOT to Include

- *Salary.* Most ads say "Send resume and salary requirements." Ignore it. At the earnings range of the job you seek, it is a no-win situation.

- *Reasons for leaving previous jobs.* These explanations are best left for the interview. If you feel compelled to mention a specific situation, you should do so in the cover letter.
- *Photograph.* Consideration of looks violates federal, state, and local employment opportunity laws, except under very limited circumstances. Unless you're planning to become an actor or model, forget it.
- *Age or race.*
- *Exaggerations.* They can be easily checked in the experience or education portion of your resume.

The Chronological or Linear Resume

A chronological resume begins with your most recent job and works backward—the same format used in job application forms. This is the resume of choice for "big ticket" managers 95 percent of the time, because:

- It supplies precise dates
- It is straightforward
- It highlights well-known or prestigious employers
- It emphasizes steady career growth
- It emphasizes current achievements first

The linear resume does the same things; it just uses a modified format. Instead of paragraphs, you list one achievement or responsibility per line.

If you have an exemplary career path, use the chronological or linear format such as those shown in Exhibits 6-1 and 6-2.

The Five Elements of a Chronological or Linear Resume

Identification

For the one to two minutes your resume is facing a prospective employer, you are on center stage. Your identifying information should be centered, with your name in capital letters or bold face (not both). Use one line each for:

- Your name. If you have a middle initial, use it. If you don't have one and have a common surname, invent one.

Exhibit 6-1. Sample chronological resume.

Ryan D. Sorenson
632 Canyon View Lane
Nashua, NH 03516-1204
(603) 555-3410

Summary: Over 12 years management and human resources experience supervising up to 20 departments responsible for more than 25,000 employees. Held senior level human relations positions ranging from high technology to Canadian federal government.

EXPERIENCE

1990–Present   RAMSDALE INTEGRATED CIRCUITRY, Nashua, NH
               Vice-President, Human Resources

Managed all human resource activities for start-up, high technology company. Supervised h.r. staff of 5. Recruited over 100 engineers and 35 administrative staff throughout New England. Interfaced with Ivy League schools for top candidates in junior engineering positions. Established policies and procedures. Directed writing and production of employee manual.

1986–1990   PUBLIC SERVICE COMMISSION, Saskatchewan, Canada
            Senior Staffing Officer

Recruited for more than 20 departments involving over 25,000 employees. Staffed positions from janitors to physicians. Counseled on stress-related issues. Implemented stress-reduction program based on Canadian medical guidelines. Developed training programs for managers, supervisors and counselors responsible for documented added productivity ranging up to 20%.

1981–1986   THOMAS LIVINGSTON COMPANY, Toronto, Ontario, Canada
            *Compensation Administration Manager and Personnel
            Supervisor*

Managed and implemented corporate plan to comply with federal government's anti-inflation program of restricted wage and price increases. Interfaced with federal officials. Made national presentations affecting 7,000 supervisors and managers of Canada's largest retail chain. Supervised testing and implementation of new management evaluation plan.

EDUCATION

B.A., Business Administration, Queen's University, Kingston, Ontario, Canada

Personal and Professional References Furnished Upon Request

Exhibit 6-2. Sample linear resume.

VIRGINIA F. MARSHALL
1378 Winston Street, #2
Los Angeles, CA 90056-0351
(213) 555-6609

Summary: Ten years management experience in major New York publishing houses. Increased marketing, administrative responsibilities throughout career.

EXPERIENCE AND ACHIEVEMENTS

1990–1994   WARNER PUBLISHER SERVICES, New York, NY
Wholesale Sales Manager, Warner Books

Served as primary liaison in all aspects of sales, marketing, and administration for the world's largest distributor of paperback books and magazines.

- Developed and implemented sales, marketing and administrative plans.
- Prepared budgets for and monitored all sales and marketing for Disney Press. Division showed a 7% gain from 1993 to 1994.
- Directed quick-turn-around sales programs for field staff.
- Represented Warner Books and Disney Press at major trade shows.

1984–1990   PENGUIN USA, New York, NY
Wholesale Sales Manager 1986–1990

Responsible for all written communications to the field force of the fourth largest publisher and distributor of books.

- Developed marketing and promotional opportunities for wholesalers for all Penguin USA imprints.
- Administered co-op advertising program with a budget of $3 million.
- Managed staff of up to four in wholesale telemarketing department. Sales increased by 12% from 1989 to 1990.

Telemarketing Supervisor 1984–1986

- Managed entire sales effort including initial and reorder business, customer service, performance tracking and marketing.
- Supervised an accounted base of 120 wholesale agencies generating dollar sales of over $3 million annually.

EDUCATION

B.S., Management Sciences concentration, Kean College, Morris, N.J.

REFERENCES FURNISHED UPON REQUEST

- Address with full spelling of "Street," "Avenue," and such. Follow with apartment or suite number, if appropriate.
- City, state, zip code. Zip should preferably have the four-digit extension. You can check it out by referring to bills from your utility company.
- Telephone number. Do not use your work number. Instead, use a home phone linked to an answering machine or voice mail. Your message on the machine should be polite, warm, but dignified. Practice smiling as you record it. Omit all background music or other sound effects. Avoid family members taking messages; it sounds unprofessional, and their messages to you may be unreliable. Don't use an answering service; you could appear to be a professional job changer.

Power Summary

Get the important facts out early. Forget about using personal information, objectives, or education on top. What you need is a concise, compelling statement that uses action language, quantifiable results, and a direct style.

[*Not This:*]

"As the public relations director for a large West Coast corporation, I have top-level experience with heavy staff advisory, policy-building, and administrative responsibility. Excellent writing and speaking skills and strong editorial background are other attributes."

[*But This:*]

"Director of Public Relations for Fortune 500 financial services corporation. Controlled budget of $5.6 million and staff of 40. Established media buying policy and revitalized corporate image."

What's wrong with the first version? It's flat. It rambles. It generalizes—"experience" and "responsibilities"—without focusing on accomplishments. It lacks positive action words like the ones contained in the second version: "directed," "controlled," "established," "revitalized." Refer to the list of action verbs in the section Writing Your Resume: Words to Use.

Experience

Center the title. You may wish to call this section Experience and Achievements since your second decade resume should highlight both. Skip a line. Begin with your most current position. Use capital letters or boldface for the following information:

- Dates (years only)
- Name of employer
- City and state (Caps or boldface are optional. Review Exhibits 6-1 and 6-2.)

There is no need for address or phone number. It will appear on the application form, if needed. Place your job title on the next line. Optionally, you may add significant facts about your employer combined into a one sentence, for example:

> "Staff accountant reporting to controller of $20 million oil exploration company."

> "Advertising manager with in-house staff of ten and annual budget of $1.25 million for twenty-nine-unit chain of optical centers grossing $25 million per year."

Beginning with the next sentence list three or four of your major accomplishments. For example:

> "Reduced media budget while significantly increasing exposure by developing in-house agency. Created and controlled $5 million promotional campaign announcing fifteen-unit expansion, leading to 10 percent increase in first-quarter sales. Negotiated, purchased, and installed five-station Desktop Publishing network, resulting in 15 percent time and cost savings."

Follow with your next most recent employer, using the identical format. Be consistent. If you've been at one job for a number of years with a variety of positions, use your Power Summary to describe the company. Then list positions in the following manner:

> 1985–1990 Vice president, marketing, headquarters, Pittsburgh, PA (followed by paragraph of achievements and responsibilities).

> 1983–1985 Sales manager, eastern region, Boston, MA (followed by paragraph of achievements and responsibilities).

Whether you've had one job or several, senior candidates are prone to go back too far. Most employers do not keep records past seven years, and few check references beyond the three most recent employers. If you have several jobs from an earlier era, consolidate with a statement like "1970–1980 Sales representative for several textbook publishing companies."

Education

A brief mention of education, without mentioning degree dates, is sufficient. For example:

> "M.S. Electrical engineering, Drexel University. B.S. Electrical engineering, Duke University"

Do not mention the year you graduated. It will "date" you as surely as if you listed your birth date. Do not indicate you received a degree if you didn't. Instead, summarize actual time spent at school, for example,

> "Three years premedical training with a major in biology."

Education is easy to check, and more employers are taking pains to find out how truthful candidates are. Getting caught in a lie is worse than omitting the information.

References

At the bottom of your resume add a phrase like "Personal and professional references furnished upon request." References are too valuable to annoy. You want to be able to contact them first and give them background on your potential employer, BEFORE the employer calls them. You also want to be able to tactfully "coach" them into providing a stand-out referral. (See Chapter 10, Turning References Into Testimonials.)

The Targeted Resume

If you know exactly the kind of position you're looking for, you may want to write a targeted resume (see Exhibit 6-3). At best, it is a supplementary resume, intended for a single use. Since its purpose is so limited, you should also have a general purpose resume. Use the targeted resume:

- When you find a specific opportunity and have the background that makes you and the position a perfect match.
- When you're applying in several fields and want a tailored resume for each.
- When you can speak the language of your career field.

Exhibit 6-3. Sample targeted resume.

HELGA CASTLE
2346 Spinning Road
West Hollywood, CA 90046-3572
(310) 555-0359

Job Target: Executive housekeeping position in major hospital.

CAPABILITIES

- Speak, read, and write English and Spanish fluently
- Prepare and implement department manuals according to JCAHO
- Reduced Workers Compensation and unemployment insurance appeals with 99% win rate at previous position
- Open and manage Obstetrics, NICU, and Immune Suppressed Units
- Direct budgets in excess of $1 million

ACHIEVEMENTS

- Developed control procedures resulting in a 15% supply reduction without impacting service
- Consistently above corporate standards for patient satisfaction; above 90% for past 7 quarters; Director of the Quarter, 4th quarter, 1993
- Received "Superior" rating from JCAHO for infectious waste management
- Participated in JCAHO survey with no adverse recommendations, 1992

EMPLOYMENT HISTORY

1989–Present   Executive Housekeeper, Downey Hospital, 182 bed acute hospital
1984–1989   Executive Housekeeper, U.S. Memorial Medical Center, Los Angeles, 377 bed acute teaching hospital
1980–1984   Director of Environmental Services, XSP (management co. for directors of food and environmental services), San Diego, CA

EDUCATION

Certificate In Administrative Housekeeping, Los Angeles Trade Technical College

References available upon request.

Do NOT use the targeted resume if you're unclear about your skills and achievements or if you have little direct experience related to your next career move.

How to Write the Targeted Resume

Although I usually don't recommend using an objective, with a targeted resume, it's desirable. Use the clearest possible language to describe exactly the position you're seeking.

Capabilities and achievements should be linked directly to your target position. Capabilities should explain what you can do for the company. Achievements should explain what you have done that worked. Use a linear format to highlight your background; use plenty of white space. Work experience follows chronologically, listing position and employer. Education and references statement complete the resume.

The Functional Resume

My instincts and professional background tell me that the chronological resume is the best format most of the time. There are exceptions. The functional resume, such as the one shown in Exhibit 6-4, may be used:

- When you're applying for a position that incorporates several different functions that mesh with a broad range of your own expertise.
- If you're considering changing careers. Then, a functional resume can define your skills across the dimensions of the new position you seek.
- If you have unexplained gaps in your employment history or have changed jobs frequently. A functional resume can "blur" the timeline. The drawback is that many employers know this ploy and don't care for it.

How to Write the Functional Resume

Begin with the same identification as in all previous resume styles. Follow with the Summary statement. The next heading is called Selected Achievements or Related Experience. On the left list four or five major subheadings, for example, Management, Planning, Manufacturing, and Technical. (These subheads can be anything that

Exhibit 6-4. Sample functional resume.

Victor L. Juarez
123 West 47th Place
Los Angeles, CA 90006-3421
(213) 555-9821

SUMMARY: Ambitious facilities engineering professional with 15 years management experience. Proficient in establishing performance goal programs to maximize efficiency in running academic and industrial facilities.

SELECTED ACHIEVEMENTS:

Performance goal program for facilities engineering, focusing on:

—Service quality improvement
—Elimination of waste
—Productivity enhancement
—Cost reductions up to 26%

Management training and development program in plant maintenance including:

—Assessing job competency
—Leadership skill development
—Performance appraisal application
—Problem solving instruction

SPECIALTIES:

Facilities engineering, management including:

—Occupancy planning
—Leased building operations
—Total quality management team building

Plant engineering/maintenance operations management including:

—Construction management and design
—Energy management
—Physical plant operations

EXPERIENCE:

1992–1993	Manager, Business Operations, Physical Plant, USC, Los Angeles
1985–1992	McDonnell Douglas, Long Beach, CA
	Manager, Facilities Planning Operations 1990–1992
	Manager, Facilities Plant Operation 1985–1990
1981–1985	Facilities/Industrial Engineer, Jason Stewart Research

AFFILIATIONS: American Institute of Industrial Engineers

EDUCATION: MBA, Pepperdine University, Malibu, CA
B.S., Business Administration, University of Arizona, Tucson

REFERENCES FURNISHED UPON REQUEST

---

pertains to your expertise, so long as they are broad enough to encompass a variety of achievements.) After each subhead, list the duties and responsibilities that fit each category. Place the most important accomplishments first.

Next list your employers in the same format as in the Targeted resume. Finish with the same sections you would use in a chronological resume—Education and References. Note that the sample resume (Exhibit 6-4) has another category called Affiliations. The resume preparer felt that his professional organizations were sufficiently important to be listed on the resume. This is a judgment call, based on your own knowledge of your career path. If it feels right, add it.

The key to getting around the deliberate vagueness of a functional resume is to use as many specific accomplishments as possible, for example, "Increased productivity by 25 percent by assigning flex hours to staff," or "Increased direct mail response by $50,000 annually." These nuggets of quantifiable results may counter the negativity often felt toward the functional resume format.

When to Use an Electronic Resume

If you plan to focus your job search on major corporations or work with on-line modem-based services and/or headhunters, you will want to modify your basic resume to adapt it to the electronic resume scanning systems. You can adapt any basic resume format. Just remember that chronological or linear is still the format of choice for larger employers.

These scanning systems are looking for labels that identify your skills and background. Generally these phrases are no more than one or two words. By defining and distilling your experience into a series of keywords (see Exhibit 6-5) you can adapt your resume to meet the newest technology. In a classic resume, you write using action words such as the verbs listed in the next section. With a keyword summary, your labels become a series of nouns that accurately pinpoint your credentials. The keyword summary goes at the top of your resume, just below the identifying materials.

In the keyword summary, you list your job title, occupation, or career field, followed by critical sales points. The remainder of the resume is basically the same as the other formats.

Other important points to remember when writing for computer readership:

Use simple basic (unfrilly) type. Avoid italic, text, script, and underlining.

Exhibit 6-5. Sample electronic resume.

KIRSTEN L. SIMMONS
451 West Temple Blvd.
Jacksonville, FL 39213-0458
(904) 555-0052

Keywords:

Loan officer. Loan department. Commercial loans. Consumer loans. Real estate loans. Collection. Bank teller. Head teller. General business. General accounting. Management. Payables. Receivables. Tax reports. Bookeeping. Bookkeeper.

Summary:

Ten years financial experience leading to position as vice president/loan administration prepared me for next major managerial position in a financial institution. Also have heavy background in roll-up-your-sleeves bookeeping for small manufacturing firm.

Experience:

1988 to Present	SEMINOLE STATE BANK, JACKSONVILLE, FL

Assistant Vice President/Loan Administration 1990–1994

Direct preparation of commercial, real estate, and construction loan documentation. Assist senior credit officer in supervising compliance and regulatory issues applicable to bank lending. Exercise approval authority within established limits of $50,000 to individuals and $100,000 to businesses. Provide collection assistance for commercial, consumer and real estate problem loans.

Bank Teller/Head Teller 1988–1990

1985–1988	RICHMOND AIRCRAFT MAINTENANCE CO., RICHMOND, VA

Managed bookkeeping functions: accounts payable, accounts receivable, payroll, tax reports for small general aviation maintenance company while attending college full-time.

Education:	B.A., Business Administration, University of Virginia, Richmond

REFERENCES AVAILABLE UPON REQUEST

Include a cover letter, because recruiters indicate they need them to amplify the resume. The letters are also electronically stored in the computer databases.

A good source for more extensive research into electronic resumes is *Electronic Resume Revolution* by Joyce Lain Kennedy and Thomas J. Morrow (New York: Wiley, 1994).

Writing Your Resume: Words to Use

Even an electronic resume needs phrases with strong action words that signal your effectiveness. For example:

"Developed a series of . . ."
"Organized a task force to . . ."
"Consistently performed . . ."
"Led a team investigating . . ."
"Managed and controlled a program to . . ."

The most effective action verbs include

accelerated	conducted	directed	identified
achieved	concluded	discovered	implemented
accomplished	constructed	dispensed	improved
administered	consulted	doubled	increased
analyzed	contracted	drafted	influenced
applied	controlled	edited	initiated
appointed	converted	eliminated	innovated
arbitrated	convinced	established	installed
arranged	counseled	evaluated	instituted
audited	cut	executed	instructed
averted	created	exhibited	introduced
budgeted	decentralized	expanded	invented
built	decided	expedited	judged
calculated	delivered	facilitated	justified
certified	demonstrated	forecasted	launched
charted	designed	formulated	led
communicated	detected	founded	maintained
compiled	determined	generated	managed
completed	developed	guided	marketed
composed	devised	handled	maximized
conceived	diagnosed	headed	measured

mediated	promoted	revitalized	tested
modernized	projected	routed	traded
monitored	provided	selected	trained
motivated	publicized	served	translated
negotiated	published	set up	traveled
obtained	purchased	simplified	trimmed
operated	raised	sold	tripled
ordered	recommended	solved	uncovered
organized	recruited	specified	undertook
oversaw	reduced	staffed	unified
packaged	referred	standardized	united
participated	regulated	streamlined	unraveled
performed	renegotiated	strengthened	used
pioneered	reorganized	studied	utilized
planned	reported	succeeded	verified
prepared	represented	summarized	weighed
presented	researched	supervised	widened
processed	resolved	supported	won
procured	responded	synthesized	worked
produced	restored	systematized	wrote
programmed	revamped	taught	

Editing Your Resume

Once you've committed your resume to paper, edit relentlessly. For best results, review it three times. On the first pass, eliminate unnecessary words, clarify ambiguities, and tighten the verbiage. For example:

> *Not* "responsible for," *but* "coordinated"
> *Not* "assisted in," *but* "directed"

On the second pass, eliminate the unnecessary and illustrate the essential. Make your resume current and relevant to today's employer's needs. Finally, proofread for spelling, grammar, and punctuation.

Give your resume to two knowledgeable people to critique. Ask them to be merciless. After they're done, review the results for final polishing.

You're not quite done. Ask several of your peers, trusted people in your network to review it and get their honest evaluation. If possible, these should be people who have exposure to top management, who can see what you are trying to accomplish.

Finally, put your resume aside for two days. Reread it one last time to make sure it profiles you properly.

What Your Resume Should Look Like

- Use plenty of white space. Have a one-inch border around the page to allow for margin notations by prospective employers. Use bullets instead of long copy blocks.
- For typesetting, use no less than 10-point size. Although 12-pitch type is acceptable in typewritten and word processing programs, resumes set in 10-point type have become the standard for most managerial and executive positions.
- If you've written your resume on a computer and have a laser printer, you may wish to print multiple copies, especially if you're doing a large mailing.
- In any case, use a conservative typeface such as Times Roman, Century Schoolbook, or Palatino. They are readable, available, and acceptable. Because they have serifs (those little squiggles on the ends of the letters) they are considered traditional and businesslike.
- Use boldface and italics sparingly. They should accent, not make your resume look like a study in multiple typefaces.
- Print your resume in black ink on quality white paper. Ivory is also acceptable, and the weight should be at least 24-pound.

That's it. Your resume should now be ready for public distribution.

A Cover Letter to Get the Resume Read

If you're sending a resume to a personnel department, don't send a cover letter. Overworked human resources types see it as just another piece of paper to shuffle.

Save your cover letter for when it counts:

- When you've scored a positive impression through a cold call and are zeroing in on the interview
- In response to a help-wanted ad

- When a reference known to you and the target employer suggests sending a resume

Target your cover letter to the decision maker. Always get a name. If possible, talk to the decision maker on the telephone briefly to learn more about the position. That way, your letter will show your knowledge of the job, with your name remembered from the call. And never use "To whom it may concern."

How to Write a Cover Letter

All effective cover letters are upbeat, concise, and direct. Your impeccable cover letter should follow sound business correspondence principles:

- Neatness counts big.
- A well-organized format enhances readability.
- Each letter should be an original, signed in black ink. Never use a photocopy.
- No letter should be more than one page long.
- Write simply. Use no compound sentences. Key points in italic or boldface are appropriate if limited to no more than five.
- Whether using a computer word processing program or typewriter, the type should be conservative. Serif fonts are preferred by business. Never use a simulated script typeface. If typewritten, use 12-pitch type.
- Margins should be 1¼ to 1½ inches around the top, bottom, and sides.

If you invest in your own letterhead (and at this stage of your career, I strongly suggest you do), use a raised black typeface and center your name, address, and telephone number near the top of the page. Order at least 24-pound, 8½-by-11-inch paper; white and ivory are the colors of choice. Print matching number 10 envelopes, with your return address (not your name), in the upper left-hand corner.

For special situations such as interview confirmations and thank-you letters following interviews, you may wish to enhance your complement of stationery with monarch size letterhead (7¼-by-11-inches) and matching envelopes. For these smaller envelopes, a return address on the back flap looks best.

If you word process or type your letter on standard blank paper, the same conservative look applies. The one difference: your address and telephone number are positioned at the top right-hand side of the page.

The Cover Letter Format

There are several ways to write cover letters. Nevertheless, they follow a specific format (review Exhibits 6-6 to 6-9).

Date is indented and two spaces directly below your address and phone number, if you are using blank paper. When using printed letterhead, the date is positioned flush right.

Your recipient's full name is flush left. Don't precede his or her name with "Mr.," "Ms.," or "Mrs." On the next line is the name of the company, without abbreviations. The next line is the address with such words as "Room" or "Suite" spelled out. The next line contains city, state, and zip code. Use the nine-digit version if you know it.

The salutation line is always positioned flush left and always addressed "Dear Mr. (or Ms.)." Never use a first name, even though you may have been told it during a telephone conversation. Don't risk using "Mrs." unless you are certain that the recipient uses it.

Skip two spaces and title the letter "Re: *Name of Position*" or "Telephone Conversation Re Interior Design Position Advertised in <u>San Francisco Chronicle</u>." (The objective is to be very specific about the nature of your first contact with the addressee.)

The body of the letter should be limited to no more than four paragraphs. Each paragraph should be no more than five lines and should begin flush left. Skip a space between each paragraph. Paragraph components include:

- *The introductory paragraph.* In this paragraph introduce yourself and briefly mention the purpose of the letter.
- *The value paragraph.* This describes the applicant's background and highlights key attributes that would benefit the company. Tone should be active and persuasive.
- *The action paragraph.* Here you ask the reader to review the resume contained and contact you. Better yet, state specifically when you will call to follow up.
- *The closing paragraph.* This paragraph expresses appreciation.

Now, skip a space. Use a complimentary closing such as "Very truly yours," "Yours sincerely," or "Best regards." Skip three more spaces and place the signature line directly below the complimentary closing line. If you are enclosing a resume or other materials along with the letter, be sure to use the word "Enclosure(s)" two spaces below your signature.

Proofread and check spelling. Never send a letter with an erasure, strikeover, or obvious white-out.

Exhibit 6-6. Sample help-wanted response letter, without letterhead.

[Note that closing and signature line up with address and date on top]

15587 Russell Street
Greenville, SC 29602-3452

December 5, 1995

Abigail N. Hardesty
Director of Human Resources
Quality Furniture Manufacturers, Inc.
1500 Magnolia Boulevard
Charleston, SC 29401

Re: Third Shift Production Manager Position

Dear Ms. Hardesty:

Your advertisement in the *Sunday Star Ledger* called for a seasoned production manager to handle third-shift operations at your Durham, North Carolina plant.

The enclosed resume reflects that I am well qualified, with over 15 years furniture manufacturing experience. After high school graduation, I began as an equipment operator, progressed through scheduling, purchasing, and inventory control to my current position as first shift production manager at Rosewood Furniture's Greenville plant. Managing Quality's larger operation in Durham is an exciting opportunity.

The "minimum educational requirements" specified in your ad were a bachelor's degree in business administration, manufacturing management, *or its equivalent.* When I began in the 1970's, a college education was not a prerequisite for rising through the manufacturing ranks. Through study and on-the-job training, I have experience in all facets of production that is probably equivalent to several college degrees.

Rotating shift schedules have hampered my ability to attend all night classes required for a degree, but I have accumulated 65 credits toward a bachelor of science in business administration, concentrating in manufacturing management. I intend to keep working until I've acquired it. I'll telephone you next week to set a convenient meeting date.

Very truly yours,

Thomas Y. Johnson

Enclosure

Exhibit 6-7.   Sample referral through mutual acquaintance letter, with letterhead.

[Note flush left stylistic format]

Sandra Y. Staunton
4632 Elgin Court
Dallas, TX 75203-3374
(602) 555-5241

June 19, 1995

Frances Chafton
MALIBU DESIGN CENTER
23805 Pacific Coast Highway
Malibu, CA 90604

Dear Ms. Chafton:

A mutual friend of ours, Cynthia McAllister at the Jennings Interior Design Center in Aubuquerque, suggested I contact you.

I have just completed the requirements for my M.B.A. degree from the University of Texas. As an undergraduate, I had the opportunity to work as a cooperative education student in the administrative offices of the Dallas Design Center. I enjoyed my work there and want to explore the possibility of combining my business management training with my interest in design.

I will be returning to my family's home in Pacific Palisades next month. Cynthia indicated you would be one of the best people to speak with regarding opportunities in the greater Los Angeles area.

I will call you next week to see whether we might schedule a meeting during the week of July 10th. I would truly appreciate it if you could take time out from your busy schedule to meet with me.

Sincerely yours,

Sandra Y. Staunton

Exhibit 6-8. Sample telephone follow-up cover letter, with letterhead.

[Note alternate paragraph format with right-hand offset date, closing and signature]

Sylvia Johnson
347 Courtney Lane
Seattle, Washington 93607-0041
(534) 555-9042

April 16, 1995

John VanCamp
Manager
FIRST WASHINGTON STATE BANK
8341 Wilson Parkway
Seattle, WA 93742

Dear Mr. VanCamp:

It was a pleasure talking with you today about your requirements for a customer service representative. You indicated that a vacancy might be pending and that another position might be newly created. As you requested, I'm enclosing a copy of my resume for your review.

During the past three years I worked as a customer service representative for U.S. Bank in Seattle. I have been responsible for answering customer inquiries, opening new accounts, promoting new banking services and handling customer complaints. I especially enjoy working with new customers to familiarize them with our services.

I would appreciate being considered for one of the above positions. I will call your offices on Friday morning to answer any questions you may have about my interests and background and to see if we might arrange a mutually convenient meeting.

Sincerely yours,

Sylvia Johnson

Enclosure

Exhibit 6-9.   Sample help-wanted response letter, with letterhead.

[Note use of bullets as an effective way to provide essential information]

Ernest P. Snow
5327 Crown Park Blvd. #204
Newport News, VA 34021
(313) 555-4303

March 17, 1995

Graham Clark
COVENTRY UNIFIED SCHOOLS
P.O. Box 35042
Columbia, SC 48351

Dear Mr. Clark:

Your recent ad in *Secondary School Administration* for a human resources ana-lyst intrigues me for several reasons. I have the necessary qualifications you outlined for this position. I'm very attracted to the Columbia area. I also be-lieve I would excel as a human resources analyst for Coventry Unified Schools.

I have acquired the following experience during my 15 years in education:

- Master's degree in psychology
- Experience in job evaluation, benefits administration, compensation analysis, performance design, and quality intervention
- Computer proficiency
- Knowledge of performance measurement and design models

I would appreciate an opportunity to interview for this position. I shall call on Thursday afternoon with a few questions concerning this position. At that time, I hope we may arrange a mutually convenient time for an interview.

Yours sincerely,

Ernest P. Snow

Keep a copy of every cover letter. You'll need them when you begin following up on your correspondence.

Once you have written your letter, ask yourself the following questions:

- Does it catch the reader's attention?
- Is it persuasive?
- Does it support the premise (to land a job interview) with evidence (your experience)?
- Does it move the reader to action?
- Does it contain the appropriate enclosures:
  —Resume
  —Supporting literature (no more than two key items). For example, a person involved in health care business operations might submit a feature article written for a trade journal that summarizes his or her views on key issues. This shows strong background in the field and immediately establishes credibility. Similarly, a journalist or graphics designer should send photocopied samples of work.

Follow-up Tactics

Be precise in targeting the arrival of your letter and resume. Tuesday through Thursday are the best days for mail to hit and make a favorable impression. Avoid sending mail so that it arrives on a Monday or a Friday.

Call within two days of your letter's arrival. If you said you'd follow up on Wednesday at 10 A.M., do so. Even if your target is not in the office or won't take your call, leave a message with your name and the purpose of the call. Find out when to call back. Then do so. If you get through, request a meeting. If you're turned down, try to get the name of another contact.

Keeping track of the resumes sent and follow-up calls is not difficult. Using a format like the one in Exhibit 6-10 will help your job-tracking progress.

The Bottom Line

Pursuing your next job should never be hit or miss. Systematically creating a resume, a series of cover letters, and then following up your leads should put you firmly in charge of your campaign.

Exhibit 6-10.   Career campaign follow-up form.

Date Sent	Type of Letter (or Resume Only)	Addressee & Company	Called On	Results

Chapter 7

Penetrating Deep Into Corporate Management

Once you have your resume in order, you should begin working on your telemarketing campaign. By now, you should have the contact names of at least a dozen likely prospects. What do you do with them?

Start With a Basic Telephone Strategy

Program your answering machine to receive any callbacks. Examples of effective messages are

> Hello. This is Judy Savage. I'm in the office today, but I'm either on the other line, or I've stepped out briefly. Please leave your name and telephone number and I'll get back to you as quickly as possible.

or

> "I'm unavailable at the moment, but this line is monitored frequently, and I will get back to you today."

The best times to check your machine for messages are 11:15 A.M. and 4:15 P.M., so you can return any calls before lunch or the end of the day.

To speak with an executive in human resources the best time to call is between 9 A.M. and 11 A.M., Tuesday through Friday. Calling on "frantic Monday" is a waste of time. Never call Friday afternoon since exit interviews are being conducted at that time.

To reach an executive other than someone in the human resources department, use the techniques described in the section in Chapter 5 entitled Efficient Personal Telephone Interviewing. Call first to learn if your target arrives at the office early. During the day, check with the executive's secretary. At night, another good information source may be the security guard who answers the corporate phones after business hours. There are other people who know who is who in the company but don't usually answer phones. Because of their isolation or "innocence" about phone techniques, you may be able to get the information from mail room personnel or shipping and receiving employees.

If your prospect arrives early, try calling before 8 A.M. when the secretary starts answering the executive's phone line.

If your targeted executive is not in, leave a message with the secretary or on his or her voice mail. Then call back at exactly the time you stated. "Hello, this is John Swift; I'm calling for Roberta Stoneman, and I will try again at 11:30 tomorrow morning." Call tomorrow at that exact time. After a few days of your repeated prompt messages, she will have been conditioned to expect your call and will be more willing to talk with you, if for no other reason than to satisfy her curiosity.

Another good time to call is after 5 P.M., when secretaries have departed. Or you can try before or after the normal lunch hour.

Why Experienced Candidates Should Try to Avoid Human Resources

- *Interviewers are usually young.* They are intake rookies who function as gatekeepers. If you call them, chances are you'll get a request for a resume. Usually, that will be the end of the line.

- *Interviewers are often unaware of high-level openings.* They don't deal in upper-level positions; or, upper management doesn't want to leak the fact that they may be looking for senior-level talent. *It's entirely possible that there may not even be a job opening* but just an idea in the CFO's mind that he wants to expand capabilities in the accounting department. When you come along after having spoken directly to the line supervisor in charge of that department, things may change rapidly in your favor.

- *Interviewers use Job Requisitions and Job Descriptions that distort actual qualifications needed.* Personnel departments work by committee. If a job requisition is placed, several people have to sign off on the order. Office politics are often injected to further muddy the waters. Alternatively, personnel may be unclear about specific job duties, but somehow they must stuff it into a specific (and possibly too low) salary range. Finally, time passes and the job configuration changes, so that by the time the job is "out there" it bears little resemblance to actual job responsibilities.

• *Hiring authorities (line supervisors or the ones who are actually working in the department you're interested in) may be coached to write the real job order around you, once you've met them.* Why? Initially, they have ill-defined wants. Still, they feel they've got to do something. You can build your own job requisition by defining what you can bring to the job. How do you achieve this?

The "Deep Breath" Phone Call

Through your earlier research, you should know the name of a specific target person in the department that matches your own job specifications. To make sure you have the necessary "credentials" to get past the gatekeeper, first send your fail-safe resume and dynamite cover letter. Then when the target's assistant asks what it's regarding, you can confidently say, "I sent a letter and resume to Mr. Johnson and want to clarify a few points."

Anyone who believes "Don't call us, we'll call you" is still waiting for the call. There is only one way to break that syndrome. Make the call. But first, prepare a miniscript on the main points you want to make.

Once you've written your self-presentation, practice it until it comes naturally to you. Read it out loud. Enlist a spouse or friend to be the other person and rehearse it. Try using a tape recorder to hear any flutters or uncertainty in your voice. You're going to put on the performance of a lifetime, guaranteed to generate a number of interviews leading to that position you have engraved in your mind's eye.

Then take a deep breath and start making the calls. The illustration that follows gives you an idea of how to position yourself. The words may vary, but your attitude shouldn't.

Four Steps for Creating an "I Can't Resist You" Script

1. Hit 'em square between the eyes with something that grabs their attention.
2. Develop a follow-through that catches their interest.
3. Strike deep with phraseology leading to a specific need to see you.
4. End with the closing that leads to *action*—that is, a request for you to come in for an interview.

Use the Attention Getter

You want to whet your prospect's attention with a quick grabber that defines who you are and what you do. Be somewhat general. Saying you have *x* years experience up front can be an instant disqualifier, for example, if you have five years in the field and the target company wants seven.

> "Hello, Mr. Sanders. My name is Ruth Dunne, and I'm a highly experienced computer sales representative for a major distributor. Have I reached you at a good time?"

Don't ever ask if you've gotten him at a *bad* time; it's too easy for him to say yes and kill the rest of the conversation. If you ask if it's a good time to speak, chances are he'll keep listening. If he says he's too busy, you can then get a follow-up time to call back.

Generate Interest—But Be Brief!

This is where your well-crafted resume comes in handy. Review it and pull out the most outstanding examples of success to date. For example:

> "Working with SFN Industries in Princeton, New Jersey, I attained 125 percent of my quota in CAD/CAM sales throughout New York and New Jersey and opened new accounts netting over $90,000 within one year."

Create the Need to See You

The company representative should be at least mildly intrigued at this point.

> "At any rate, Mr. Sanders, I'm looking for a new challenge. Based on what I already know about your company, especially the new product lines I read about in the *Wall Street Journal,* I feel we may have some basis for discussion."

You can also remind him,

> "I sent you a resume last week that further explains my qualifications."

Don't Forget the Closer

Your presentation should end with a question that leads to the bottom line, "Is my experience and background what you might be looking for on your staff?"

This is deep breath time for you. What you'll probably hear on the other end is silence as your target digests what you've told him. At this point, you can expect one of three responses:

"I'm interested. Let's get together." Great! All you have to do is set the appointment time.

"What are you earning? Do you have a degree?" These further questions that show some interest can be finessed to yield the interview.

"Gee, I don't remember your resume. Let me check it out first and I'll get back to you." Warning: This one probably won't fly. There is one small window of opportunity left. You may counter with "Is there another time I should call you back?"

Turning Negative Responses Into Positives

You've put your best foot forward and your pride on the line. Still, out of all the calls you make, many are bound to be brush-offs or ringing with negative vibes. Here are some proven techniques to turn them around:

- "You need to speak to human resources about that." Say, "Of course, Mr. Johnson, to whom shall I speak and what specific position shall I mention?" What you have gained from this is:
  —Insight on a specific job opening
  —An opportunity to say to the human resources manager "Mr. Johnson suggested we speak about the senior purchasing agent's position."
  —A second chance to present your credentials: Even if the young personnel type doesn't know about the senior purchasing agent position, you can be sure he'll get the update from Mr. Johnson. You may have to resend your resume to human resources at this point. This time enclosing a cover letter is appropriate, since you can refer to "my recent conversations with Mr. Johnson and Mr. Light in human resources."

- "I'm too busy right now." This is one of the easier responses to counter. It works best with a considerate response that shows your empathy, plus a couple of probing questions: "Of course; sure sounds like you could use some help! I'd like to try you in a week or so. Are mornings or afternoons better for you?" He has to respond to the question affirmatively—even if only to get you off the phone.

Or, you can be a bit bolder and say: "I'll be near your offices on Wednesday. Perhaps I can come by then for a few minutes. Would morning or afternoon be better?" If your target is still too busy, back down gracefully and say: "I certainly do understand. I'll try you again in a week or two and see if the timing is better." Obviously, you can't push a truly recalcitrant or negative target to the limits. You're merely extending the option for a "maybe" interview to become a "yes."

- *"We just don't need anyone right now."* What can you salvage from this obvious turndown? Be gutsy enough to ask for a referral.

> "Does your company have any other divisions that may be able to use someone with my background?"
>
> "Do you know someone in the business community who might have a lead for me?"
>
> "Do you know any other rapidly growing companies in the field?"
>
> "When do you anticipate an opening in your company?"

You can conclude by saying, "I've heard so many good things about XYZ Bearings, I'd like to keep you on my list. May I call you back within a few months?"

Assuming your concerted job search lasts for a few months, there is nothing wrong with reexamining old leads once sufficient time has passed. The key, of course, is to keep accurate records.

The "Voice of Experience" Phone Call

Another way to sidestep the human resources department is to draw on two elements you already possess: (1) Knowing who and when to call within the correct department (based on your early research) and (2) your own personal expertise, because you're going to call and offer your services as a consultant. It's accepted practice for consultants to discuss projects directly with those responsible for them.

What do you need to be a consultant?

- An age from mid-30's upward
- A judicious, wise appearance
- Conservative garb

- An ability to pronounce at least twenty of the latest buzzwords in your field, which you can glean from trade publications
- A business card
- Your "can't miss" resume and optionally a basic brochure about your expertise and services

Consulting is a fail-safe technique to get to your target because it gets you in the front door to talk with the real hiring authority. It positions you immediately to talk with the person making decisions without alienating the personnel department.

Consulting is so easy to discuss because there is almost no expense or risk to the "client." As an independent contractor rather than employee, you are not on the books for all those expensive benefits. When you make your call and you are asked what you charge, you say, "There's no charge unless I can be of specific assistance. Why don't we meet to find out?"

The usual telephobia will subside after a few calls. A competent advisor listens well, probes, ask questions, and uses the same vocabulary as the client. You view the appointment as an end in itself. The call is the means—and it usually takes about five minutes to arrange. Any longer reduces chances for an interview.

Typical Dialogue for the "Voice of Experience" Call

RECEPTIONIST: Good morning, Company X.

YOU: Hi. What's the name of your director of finance?

RECEPTIONIST: We don't have a director of finance. Would you like to speak to our chief accountant?

YOU: Yes, please. What's her name?

RECEPTIONIST: Gail Davis. One moment, I'll ring.

SECRETARY: Accounting. May I help you?

YOU: Hi. Ms. Davis, please.

SECRETARY: May I tell her who's calling?

YOU: [*Your first and last names.*]

SECRETARY: May I tell her what it's regarding?

YOU: Sure, I wanted to speak to her about your cost control system.

SECRETARY: Is there something I can help you with?

YOU: No, I'm sorry. I really must speak with Gail.

SECRETARY: Just a moment. I'll see if she's available.

GAIL: Gail Davis.

YOU: Hi, Gail. My name is ＿＿＿＿＿＿＿. I'm a consultant in the finance area and would like to discuss how I might assist you with improving your cost control system.

GAIL: Our system works fine. Well, a few things could use improvement.

YOU: I'm really familiar with this and have been very successful in reducing costs with clients. What areas do you see as needing improvement?

GAIL: Inventory control has really become a problem. We're just unable to keep track of our costs!

YOU: Your costs? Why?

GAIL: Well, our production control group has not been following up on status reports.

YOU: An objective appraisal can often help to straighten this problem out.

GAIL: Really? I never thought of that.

YOU: I'll be in your area on a consulting assignment later this week. Why don't I stop by at nine on Thursday morning?

GAIL: I'm on a very limited budget. What do you charge?

YOU: Why don't we see whether I can be of assistance first. There won't be any charge at all. If I can do you some good, we can discuss it further. However, it appears we'll be able to reduce the costs substantially at Company X without a major change.

GAIL: OK. You're on.

YOU: Thanks. I estimate we'll be about an hour.

GAIL: Fine.

YOU: I'm looking forward to meeting you. See you then.

GAIL: Sounds good. Bye.

YOU: Goodbye.

While the call can start differently and take an infinite number of turns, you are controlling the dialogue. It should be a dialogue, *not* two monologues. Listen actively, but don't give away your valuable advice when clients are willing to pay for it.

Rules for the "Voice of Experience" Phone Call

- You might not reach your target on the first call. Always leave your name: "John Acton, counselor on cost containment." Leave your phone number.
- If your target calls back, be courteous, but "too busy" to talk. Ask if you can return the call in a few minutes. Then collect your thoughts, review your notes, and relax. By calling back, you are in a position of control.
- Utilize a basic principle of success: "You get what you want, if you give others what they want."

- Don't mention that you are looking for a job. Remember, the interview is an end in itself.
- For optimum results, schedule appointments one hour after the start of business. Avoid making consultant appointments after lunch. By the afternoon, the supervisor is probably running behind on morning projects, sluggish from lunch, and preoccupied.

The Interview Confirmation Letter

Using a consistent program of phone prospecting, you should be setting interviews into the following weeks. For all but the hottest opportunities that beckon you to "Come in tomorrow," you should respond with a quick follow-up letter (see Exhibit 7-1).

Its purpose is to fix the appointment date in the interviewer's mind, to make you stand out from the pack, and to show that you understand the degree of professionalism that an upper-tier position requires.

Allow at least three days for a same-city letter to arrive. Anticipate at least a week if the letter is going beyond a 200-mile radius or out of state.

Your stationery should be white or ivory, preferably imprinted with your name, address, and telephone number. Monarch size letterhead (7¼-by-11-inch) with matching envelopes is ideal for this type of correspondence. Otherwise, use your regular letterhead.

The approach should be short and to the point. The first paragraph should thank the prospect for the opportunity to meet with him/her. Then it should confirm the time and location (but not the address), for example, "in your office" or "in the boardroom at General Life Insurance Company." The final paragraph reiterates that you are enclosing your resume. (If you've sent one before, and your prospect remembers it, don't bother. You can say, "As you recall, you have my current resume on your desk." Otherwise, send it.) If your interviewer has requested that you bring supporting materials, mention that you will have them at the interview.

A simple "Sincerely yours," concludes the letter.

Exhibit 7-1. Sample Interview Confirmation Letter.

Veronica J. Blessings
245 Pierce Road, #304
Norfolk, VA 23415
(202) 555-1934

April 27, 1995

Lawrence Joyner
Business Manager
GREATER WASHINGTON D.C. CONVENTION CENTER
2484 Pittsburgh Avenue
Washington, D.C. 20536

Dear Mr. Joyner:

Thank you for the opportunity to interview for the catering manager's position at the Greater Washington D.C. Convention Center. I look forward to meeting with you in your offices next Wednesday, at 9:30 A.M.

Because you indicated that you had passed my original resume on to Mr. Jenkins in your offices, I am enclosing another for your files. Please let me know if you need any additional information prior to our meeting.

Sincerely yours,

Veronica J. Blessings

Enclosure

Chapter 8

Interviewing With Experience

So far, so good. Your resume has opened the door for you. But it won't win the job on its own. Over 95 percent of people are hired on the basis of one (but usually more) interviews. Often, the more responsible the job, the more fences to hurdle.

The information in your resume—your experience, skills, schooling—has made you a candidate. The real measure of success—the main reason for the hire—is how they like you.

Most people agree that first impressions really count. Those impressions are even more important when you're in mid career, because hiring authorities see so many people for fewer available positions. Personnel policy says they're not supposed to discriminate. Law says they may not. Consciously, they probably don't want to discriminate. But that's what they're paid to do. They stereotype, so although you may seethe with individualism, that first impression had better conform to what they expect.

My own experience proves this. When I began my career, the location was just a converted house next to the main building.

My supervisor's office was in front, and I had an airless cubbyhole behind. He'd see the applicants. We didn't need resumes, applications, or references to decide. He'd buzz me on the intercom and say, "This one looks good," or "How about that loud shirt?" True to form, 95 percent of the time, the one he *liked* was the one who got the job.

Should you throw out all the rest of your carefully crafted plans for an interview and concentrate only on your looks? Of course not. It's like a great watch. To get them to appreciate your fine internal works, you'd better be sure the exterior case is polished to as near perfection as possible.

What to Wear for the Interview

The Move-Up Checkup for Men

Look critically at your interviewing wardrobe as it exists today. You've been around for at least a decade. Your wardrobe shouldn't look as if it had fought all the battles with you. Are there pulls in the fabric, frayed cuffs on the jackets, or is there a slight shine to the seat of your pants? Are the buttons about to drop off your dress shirts, or have one-too-many wearings made them dingy with age?

Give yourself a move-up checkup. The way you look is most important in your marketing strategy. Improving your looks is much easier and more fun than improving your credentials or disposition.

Be tough on yourself. Why do you think aspiring actors, politicians, and lawyers look like people at the top. They know this simple truth: "Look the part, and the part plays itself."

Now's the time to invest in a few good new items and label them "For interview only" until you're where you want to be.

Where to go? A first-class store that will coordinate suit, shirts, and ties. Don't forget about new black shoes. Run-down-at-the-heels shoes label you as run down. Have the suit tailored so it really fits. Don't cut corners here. Even though most stores no longer throw in major tailoring, it's important to look your impeccable best.

Another option that's a great money saver if you live near a major city is to check out their cut-rate garment district. The direct-selling competitive surroundings usually makes the buys unbeatable. Cash only may prevail in some stores, so be prepared. Nearby tailors may charge less than half the usual rates.

A tip: Wear comfortable walking shoes, but take the shoes you plan to wear with your new clothes to verify heel height. It's tough to tailor correctly when you're wearing Reeboks or Nikes. Also, take a shirt that can provide for accurate measurements, like how much cuff to show.

One more savings opportunity is the out-of-town manufacturers discount malls, which are becoming more prevalent. It's likely you'll have to take your purchases for tailoring closer to home, but the savings can be substantial.

A Man's Interviewing Uniform

No secret here. The uniform hasn't changed much since you got your first major job.

- Suit—Dark, conservative, preferably navy blue. Single breasted. Subtle pattern, if any. Wool and wool blends look better and last longer. Save gray for the second interview. Lead with the dark blue suit and you're more likely to be back in the gray one.

- Shirt—White, fresh from the laundry, and starched. Wear a clean one for each interview. You can keep a spare in your car or even your briefcase for the day's second interview. Wear an up-to-date collar style and if you choose French cuffs, avoid cufflinks that are large, garish, or that display religious, service, or fraternal organizations.

- Tie—Dark, striped. Again, blue is best. A contrasting color like red is OK, but the predominant color should match your suit. Silk or other thin fabrics rank highest in interview fashion sense.

- Hair—Make sure it's always clean. Avoid the greasy or wet look. For body and volume use a brush and hair dryer simultaneously. With few exceptions, neat, conservative, natural-looking hair is the rule. Keep your sideburns trimmed and the back of your neck shaved between haircuts. Length should be no longer than the bottom of your neck. If your stylist isn't up-to-date, find a new one.

What about that bald spot? Better to be honest and let it show than to try to comb a flap over from the other side. It just looks funny, not better. What about a toupee or other hair replacement? If you're investing in a good one, it's your call. But be certain it's believable. And remember—if you anticipate swimming or jogging with members of the office staff before or after hours, forget it.

- Face—Wear a beard or moustache only if the top executives do. Keep an electric razor in your briefcase and duck into a public restroom for a fresh-up if your day runs long. Glasses should be a conservative, current style.

- Hands—A professional manicure is not necessary, but keep your nails trimmed and clean. A buffer is a good investment, or use clear nail polish. A ring should be simple in design and expensive in looks. Since a watch is hidden by your suit jacket, it doesn't matter as much. (Successful second-decaders tend to wear gold and eat with silver.)

- Fragrance—Use sparingly or not at all. The sense of smell is the most basic of all the senses. It's a thousand times stronger than taste. The receptors in the nostrils of your interviewer are directly connected to the part of his brain that is involved with his deepest emotions. You don't want him to remember how the uncle who teased him unmercifully wore your kind of aftershave or set off his allergies with your scent. Better to go easy; better yet, forget it.

Interview Grooming for Women

Image consultants don't agree on an interviewing uniform for women in career ascendancy. They do agree that conservative attire is best and that suits or dresses in basic colors are appropriate.

- The basic look—Limit your creativity to fabrics, patterns, and cuts. Pure wool and linen look good initially, but both wrinkle. Combinations of natural and synthetic fabrics may pay off in better shape retention. If you choose a blend, be careful with polyester because it can look cheap to the trained professional eye. A wool blend is usually your best choice.

Where men can safely go only as far as solids or pinstripes, for women a small plaid pattern is attractive and acceptable.

Skirt lengths rise and fall, fall and rise. Yours should rise only to kneetop and lower to just below kneecap. That range is always safe; where it falls for you depends on your comfort level.

What colors should women choose? Charcoal gray—medium to steel, black, and navy blue. Colors to avoid: brown and tan. They are unprofessional, "plodding worker" tones.

- Blouses—Long sleeves generate greatest authority. Avoid V-necks and sleeveless styles at all costs. White or pale blue are most universally accepted. There is a slight leeway to pink or gray if the organization is a bit more creative. Bows, conservative collars, or asymmetrical closing blouses work well with jackets.

- Shoes—Shoes should be real leather (plastic squeaks), simple and with moderate heels, in a dark color to match or complement your clothing. They should be polished and clean.

- Hosiery—It should be new and a neutral color. Keep an extra pair of pantyhose in your purse or briefcase for emergency changes.

- Jewelry—If worn, it should be kept to a minimum. Good, simple gold and silver accessories are OK. Use no flashy fashion jewelry. Like men, you should wear no jewelry reflecting religious or organizational affiliations. Earrings should match your other jewelry and be no larger than the size of your earlobe.

- Purse—It should not be too large, nor overstuffed, and should coordinate with the color of your shoes. Real leather is best.

- Hair—As with men, your hair frames your face. Shorter is better. If yours is longer than the bottom of your neck, pin it back or wear it up. Otherwise, you run the risk of wanting to look like a little girl, when you should know better.

Color is a personal preference, but should look natural in appearance. Don't go back to a dark brown or black if a few grey hairs are beginning to show. Opt for a shade slightly lighter than your natural color. It hides the years best. If you're blonde, highlights are great. Avoid the monochromatic flash in the platinum and silver tones.

- Face—Makeup should be understated and natural. If you want to incorporate a new, fresh look, I suggest you go to a department store where they have "consultants" (read: commission sales help) and do some experimenting. Their practical experience with so many items and their insights from the manufacturers will generally help you.

Tell them you need a basic daywear look. Don't let them try any heavy/dark shadows better suited for nights at a club. With your basic information tucked safely in your head, resist the temptation to buy. Go to your nearest drugstore or beauty supply store and get what you need cheaper. The best least busy times to hit the department stores are weekdays or evenings, except before major holidays.

In eyeglasses, there's enormous variety. Here again, avoid outdated, outlandish, or oversized styles.

- Hands—You want to look as if you can attack a keyboard without fear of breaking a nail, even if you'll have a secretary handling all computer work for you. Go conservative. Nails should extend no longer than one-quarter inch past the fingers, and should be polished in traditional muted shades. Invest in a good manicure, if you can afford it.

- Fragrance—Don't douse yourself in perfume, but do wear a light scent. The selection should be carefully made and changed only rarely since the subliminal "power of a woman" is being created and maintained. As with makeup and dress, moderation is the key, but it's not a negative to be attractive and feminine.

The Finishing Touch for Both Sexes

For both women and men regardless of position, a briefcase or attaché case is an excellent accessory. Burgundy or brown is OK for women. Men should choose black, because it matches their shoes. The case should be wide enough to contain a small container of instant coffee (with caffeine) or a few regular tea bags (I'm about to explain why), mouthwash, deodorant, nonsmoking tablets (if necessary), a comb or brush, a gold pen with black ink, a legal pad, six extra copies of your resume, and a few samples of your written or published work, if appropriate. The last item should be a completed application form. Call any employer and get a standard application form sent to your home. Fill it out and have it with you so you can transfer all necessary information to the form in the office you visit. Another option: Call the human resources department of your target employer to obtain the application. With enough time before the interview, you can neatly type it.

Above all, spend extra time on your general grooming before the interview. That includes a hot shower or bath. Avoid foods likely to offend if eaten before you arrive. Most important, stay cool. Like the old TV commercial says, "Never let them see you sweat."

What to Eat Before the Interview

In addition to the right clothing and mental preparation, you need the right internal balance. You should appear at an interview rested and relaxed. The right food and beverage properly fuel your interviewing engine. I strongly recommend coffee to keep you alert. Caffeine has a predictable, positive, harmless effect. It causes neurons in brain cells to fire faster and helps you store and retrieve information readily. It's also a metabolism booster that raises your energy level. Both of these effects improve your delivery.

If coffee disagrees with you, try regular tea instead. It's less powerful but has fewer side effects. Over-the-counter tablets have higher levels of caffeine, and you don't want to appear jumpy.

Eat a light snack about half an hour before the interview to help avoid a growling stomach or a sudden drop in blood sugar that can make you lethargic or snappy. The perfect snacks are the prepackaged cheese and peanut butter cracker sandwiches. They contain just the right proportion of carbohydrates, protein, and bulk. The salt reduces the diuretic effect of the coffee, so you won't have to leave for the restroom as the offer is being extended. Avoid fruit and candy; they accentuate the drop in blood sugar levels.

Pack a small bottle of red (cinnamon) mouthwash. It's much more effective than other types. Forget breath mints and gum. They don't work.

Arriving at the Interview

When to Arrive and Where to Go First

You want to appear on time at the interview. Plan to arrive an hour early. Trust me—you have plenty to do.

For the first half hour, take an unguided sightseeing tour of the area. If it's a suite in an ordinary office building, casually walk or drive around. Get the feel of the area. Have your coffee or tea and crackers. Be friendly to the people you meet, but avoid anything that distracts you for more than a minute or so.

If the business occupies the entire building or a major floor, you're in luck. Look at bulletin boards and other directories. Observe the people. Strike up a conversation with the security guard (an excellent source of information). As you wait for the elevator, try to get a feel for employee conversations. Finally, review your notes on this employer, two or three times.

What to Do Before Entering the Waiting Room

With twenty to thirty minutes to go, get your bearings. Try to strike up a conversation and ask plenty of questions. Learn about the company history, philosophy, employees, buzzwords, and events. This is a bonanza for an observant listener. Just don't get involved in anything that will take more than a few minutes.

With about fifteen minutes to go, find the restroom and "rest." Close the door on the stall and rest. Take a deep breath and relax. Imagine yourself winning the job.

Get up, check yourself in the mirror, freshen up, and practice your best smile. You should have completed the job application before you arrive. Now, chin up, shoulders back, feet straight forward, feeling confident, self-assured, and poised, check in with the receptionist. Introduce yourself professionally and state who you are there to see. Then give the receptionist your neatly typed application.

If your appointment is with the department supervisor or other executive, the same routine applies. In this case, only your resume may be necessary.

The curtain is about to go up. It's almost your moment to star.

Dos and Don'ts

Remove any outerwear and hang it in the reception area. If no hangers are provided, ask the receptionist to store it for you. Holding a coat or other item physically distances you from the interviewer, causes you to juggle items, and disrupts your train of thought.

Don't wear sunglasses. Your shades will be interpreted as "shady" or just "too trendy." You need to make direct eye contact.

What if you're on time and the interviewer is late? Politely tell the receptionist you cannot wait more than fifteen minutes, and ask that the message be transmitted immediately to the interviewer. Even if it's an unavoidable, unintentional delay, you're better off not waiting. You'll be angry, irritable, and dropping from the psychomotor peak (helpful stage fright) reached at the scheduled time.

If you choose to stay and see it through, consider it a dress rehearsal. It is—you won't get hired.

Greeting the Interviewer

Interpersonal communications research indicates that nearly 70 percent of all hiring decisions are made on the basis of nonverbal communications. When verbal comments and nonverbal clues are compared, nonverbal traits are seen as more credible, because they're more difficult to control. It all goes back to the old saying that "Actions speak louder than words."

Having said that, I'm going to show you how those nonverbal signals can be controlled to your best advantage.

Before entering the room to meet and greet, take three deep breaths—inhaling and exhaling slowly. This relaxes you for what's about to follow, because the first five minutes of any interview are more significant than all the rest.

The Magic Four Greeting

When meeting the interviewer, you need to do four things virtually simultaneously. (Practice makes perfect; so practice until it seems natural and sincere.)

1. *The smile.* It doesn't come just from your mouth but from deep down inside. Imagine telling your favorite person, "Honey, I got the offer," and you'll smile genuinely, all right. As you smile from time to time during the interview, it should be enough to carry through a positive attitude but not so much that you're not taken seriously.

2. *Eye contact.* Make it straightforward, friendly, and assured. Later on you can and should use direct eye contact frequently as you ask and answer questions. People perceive those who can look them in the eye as trustworthy. By averting your head, you transmit a shifty, insincere image. Temper the eye contact with moderation. You don't want to stare down the interviewer so hard that he or she feels uncomfortable.

3. *Words to use.* Simply say, "Hi, I'm [*first and last name*]. It's a pleasure meeting you."

4. *The handshake.* Aside from making the Magic Four flow naturally, a proper handshake is often hardest to master. The handshake sets the tempo for the interview. If you have a fearsome grasp or a moist, sweaty palm, practice shaking hands with your other hand. It all gets back to body language. In *Contact: The First Four Minutes*, Leonard Zunin devoted an entire chapter to handshakes. He writes:

> . . . at one large company . . . [the] personnel director told me that regardless of the qualifications of a man he interviews, if his handshake is weak and clammy, he's out. Such reaction to body language is far more prevalent than we realize as others assume many things about our glance, stance or advance.

As a woman, your handshake should be firm and forthright, not overly dainty and restrained.

If you're a man and your interviewer is a woman, one of the quickest turnoffs is to shake her hand so strongly that her rings dig into her palms. You'll be out the door with no reprieve, as she recalls the painful start of your interview.

Starting the Interview

What to Avoid

Don't address the interviewer by his or her first name—not on the telephone, in any correspondence, nor in person. It should always be "Mr." or "Ms." If the interviewer calls you by your first name, ask if you may reciprocate. "Mr. Kenton, may I call you Howard?" Don't assume a submissive role. Showing deference and respect is one thing. Acting like Casper Milquetoast is another. It's natural to go slowly in strange new circumstances, but crawling won't win the job. When you put your best foot forward, your body and mind generally follow.

Phrases That Prevent Job Offers

Even with ten years on the job, you might have a tendency to reflect on how things were in the "good old 1980s." Forget that mental imagery, along with any dusty, tired, condescending lines, or any type of sexist or discriminatory language like:

"At my age. . . ."
"Back in the days when. . . ."

"Nowadays. . . ."
"The girls in the office. . . ."
"When I was younger. . . ."
"When I was your age. . . ."
"It used to be that. . . ."

Don't call the interviewer "honey" or "dear." Don't refer to grown women as "gals" and men as "guys." Aside from being offensive, these prejudicial phrases are fatal for several not-so-obvious reasons.

- *Subliminal power considerations.* Such language puts you in a dangerous, defensive position. You want to lead from a position of personal power. As Herb Cohen, author of *You Can Negotiate Anything*, points out: "Power is based upon perception. If you think you've got it, then you've got it. If you don't think you have it, even if you've got it, then you don't have it." You can and should be calm, straightforward, and unpretentious, yet still project that you've got it.

- *Generation gap considerations.* It's quite possible you'll be interviewed by someone younger than you are. That's OK. Just don't use language, tone, or intimation that suggests that the two of you are so far apart that you have nothing in common. You do. He or she wants to "get that damn position filled" and you know you're the best candidate for it.

- *Hirer job security considerations.* When you're interviewing with a department head, you certainly don't want to say anything that will imply you're after his job. Better to emphasize the role of team player with phrases like,

> "As far as future promotion goes, that depends on my working
> with a manager who wants me to grow. I can take direction well,
> and I love to learn new things."

Where and How to Sit

If there is a sofa, stand until asked to be seated. With both of you sitting on the sofa, you create an atmosphere of "You and me against the job requirements" rather than you against me.

If the interview is at a desk, commonly there will be two chairs facing the interviewer. If possible, sit on your favored side (usually your right), and to the interviewer's left. Or sit where the interviewer will be on the most advantageous side of you. Your ability to control the interview will be greatly enhanced.

Look for an opportunity to walk around to the interviewer's side during the interview, so you can look at some report or project *together.*

To convey interest in the discussion, sit with an almost imperceptible lean toward the interviewer.

What to Do

Admire something in the interviewer's office but not a personal item like a family picture or piece of apparel. It should be something neutral like a plaque or a desk accessory. It buys you time to assess the interviewer's style in those few moments while greetings are exchanged and seats are taken.

How to Assess the Interviewer's Style

Communication authorities categorize personalities according to specific traits. If you read certain clues given by the individual and his or her environment you can decide how to proceed.

1. *Outgoing and direct.* How to spot this type:

   - Flamboyant style of dress. Even in a conservative office, he or she might wear a bright tie or scarf. Prefers current fashion to classic styles.
   - Keeps plenty of mementos in the office.
   - Maintains a cluttered or, at least, a covered desk.
   - May keep you waiting, because he or she is juggling so much.

These kinds of interviewers are "people people." They gravitate toward personnel positions. If you're conservative or reserved, you can get into trouble with this kind of interviewer. You'll have to smile more and get to the point faster. They have to like you before they'll listen to you. And they're not big on listening. If you are this type, be careful. You don't want to outtalk, outsmile, or outinterview the interviewer.

2. *Self-contained and direct.* Unlike Type 1 "socializers," Type 2s are far more reserved and conservative. Until the advent of computer whiz kids who run companies, general wisdom viewed Type 2s as the epitome of top management. They're still among high achievers. How to spot this type:

- Impeccable tailoring, impeccably worn.
- Well-organized work space, with a few expensive personal desk accessories. Perhaps one or two classic picture frames containing family photos. Nothing flashy. Totally understated.
- A firm handshake but few words and not much of a smile. They'll size you up critically as they wait for you to commit the first gaff.
- Time conscious to the point of annoyance if you're late.
- Goal- and bottom-line oriented.

Don't try to joke around here. Be all business, but don't let him or her intimidate you. If he pounces on weaknesses in your background, just explain them by turning them into strengths.

3. *Self-contained and indirect.* These are the "thinkers." They're lone wolves who don't speak up, socialize, or editorialize, but they get their work done properly. How to spot this type:

- Uninteresting, understated clothes with grey and beige predominating. Practicality reigns supreme.
- Few, if any, personal items on desk.
- An organized desk; may have a to-do list, with items neatly crossed off.
- Generally a limp handshake.
- Time conscious and work oriented. The thinker's work ethic is as strong as the director's, but he or she doesn't want to run things.

Quiet and self-effacing, this person is hard to draw out, and he or she may become annoyed if you try. Pushy, aggressive behavior won't work. Answer questions directly and succinctly, and volunteer as much information as he or she needs to make a decision. This interviewer thrives on data but needs time to analyze it. So don't rush.

4. *Outgoing and indirect.* An apt description is "helpers," who are friendly like socializers, but without the aggressiveness. They take time to know you before the actual interview begins. They're nice but will do almost anything to avoid making a decision. How to spot this type:

- Nonthreatening appearance. Neutral shades, soft fabrics.
- Numerous personal items on his or her desk—often handmade.
- Friendly, expressive, and concerned approach. May apologize for keeping you waiting as he or she solves everyone else's problems. Will smile warmly and reach out to take your hand.

- Ringing phone, work piling up, and many uncompleted projects. To this interviewer, people are all that matter.

This person is the opposite of the "director." You'll never find him or her in the executive office. To get hired, take time to establish rapport, become friends, and accentuate the person part of you. Remember to limit your interview to forty-five minutes.

With a helper, it's your responsibility to get your job qualifications across. The interviewer won't ask you for a reason to hire you or even recommend you for a second interview, because he thinks of you as his *friend*.

How to Exploit the Personality Type System

Learn the system and use it to out-stereotype the stereotypers. Some will fit the description exactly. Others will fit several. Study various types of your friends to practice picking up the clues to someone else's *predominant* personality style. Then practice playing to them.

Picking up clues from a person's appearance, speech, and body language will serve you well throughout your career.

Use Body Language to Maximum Effectiveness

In the nonverbal cues you send out, nothing says more about you than how you carry yourself. The old rule Mom told you about "Chin up and shoulders back" means more than good posture.

In *Live for Success*, John Malloy writes that the "look that most impresses interviewers is a bearing of upper middle class." What this means is:

- Keep your shoulders back and head erect.
- Don't fold your arms across your chest.
- Don't sit with legs or arms wide apart.
- Use gestures to enhance your spoken message.
- Nod your head affirmatively at appropriate times, but don't overdo it. This gives positive nonverbal feedback to the interviewer.
- Speak clearly; no mumble-mouths need apply.
- Pause for emphasis.
- Don't speak too fast or too slowly.
- Become a good listener. Make it obvious that you are paying close attention to the conversation.

Pacing: Best Technique to Align With the Interviewer

Will Rogers said, "I never met a man I didn't like." Jeff Allen says, "Neither did I. That's why I never saw a job I couldn't get."

Do you know people who have a knack for getting any job they want, when they want it? Want to know their secret? It's nothing mysterious. They simply learned that liking their interviewer has a dramatic, positive effect. It involves a powerful basic motivational rule: *People like people who like them.*

An employment interview is a place to be liked. Otherwise, you won't get hired.

As I wrote in *How to Turn an Interview Into a Job*:

> Pacing is an accepted psychological technique which has been developed to increase rapport with others. It stems from an even more powerful law of human motivation, "We like people who are like ourselves." If you think about it, our entire hiring process is guided by that law.

So is almost every other determination we make about others. Think about how you vote, select friends, make television and radio choices, or buy goods and services. Pacing means aligning yourself with the overlooked and overworked interviewer, then leading (steering) her slowly but surely into extending the offer.

In short, you need a common ground before you can move to a common goal. Whether you call it pacing, alignment, identification, or empathy doesn't matter. When you meet someone from a different generation or with a different vocabulary, gestures, values system, or lifestyle, you must modify and adapt their traits to suit your own style.

Combine Pacing With Mirroring

Pacing is among the most potent job-clinching techniques ever developed. Once seated in your most favorable position, you need to *mirror* the interviewer's body language, eye movement, facial expressions, tone of voice, rate of speech, and rate of breathing.

Notice I said mirror, *not* mimic. It takes practice to get it right. But the results will amuse and amaze you. This subtle form of imitation is an absolute way to establish rapport. Just be certain to align, *not* offend.

So successful is mirroring that the best telemarketers even learn to do it on the telephone.

The Language of Interviewing

Use Insider Language

The primary use of insider language is to lock in your alignment with the interviewer. It's a linguistic password that gets you into his or her thought processes and permits you to lead. It also signifies your compatibility with the corporate culture.

Company buzzwords should be noted in your job search research and used properly.

As for employment buzzwords (near and dear to any hirer's heart), here's what you need:

Acceptance   Easiest response to any job offer. "When do I start?"

Available labor pool   What you are walking on, rather than swimming in.

Contact information   Your name, address, and telephone number(s).

Internal referral   Someone working for your potential employer who will act as your public relations representative.

Involuntary termination   Generally refers to layoffs and termination for cause.

Job compatibility   Similarity between what you've done and what the employer anticipates you'll be doing. Even if they appear totally different, 90 percent or more of every job is comparable.

Job congruence   The extent to which the job being offered meets what you want to do. Your attitude should be that they are identical, or congruent.

Job description   An internal list of duties of a particular position. Looks good on paper, but tells you more about the person who wrote it than the job itself.

Job order   Authorization to a placement service containing a summary of the position, salary range, and type of individual sought. Generally bears no similarity to person hired.

Job rotation   A system in which some employers designate certain employees to rotate jobs, so each learns the functions of a certain activity.

Labor grade   A device used in wage and salary administration to rank jobs in their order of value and compensation.

New start (new hire)   What you will be on your first day at Company X.

Offer   Something you receive as a result of packaging and selling yourself properly.

Personal/professional references   See Chapter 10 for all you need to know.

Rate range   A device used in wage and salary administration to determine the lowest and highest amount that will be paid for a specific job.

Requisition (rec)   The form initiated by a supervisor to obtain approval for hiring. Once the approval cycle is completed, it becomes an open requisition (open rec).

Span of control   The number of subordinates a supervisor can handle effectively.

Voluntary termination   One of two ways employment is severed. Usually occurs as the result of finding a better position—your next goal.

Develop an Action Vocabulary

The winners in life use certain words. If you use them, you'll sound, look, and even begin to feel like a winner. Is it an act? Who cares, if it works?

Dennis Waitley wrote in *The Psychology of Winning*, "Perhaps the most important key to the permanent enhancement of self-esteem is the practice of positive self-talk. Every waking moment we must feed ourselves subconscious self-images, positive thoughts about our self-image and our performance. . . . Winners rarely 'put themselves down' in actions or words."

The Most Potent Words to Add to Your Waking and Working Vocabulary

ability	direct	improve	reliable
accelerate	discipline	incisive	responsible
accurate	drive	innovate	results
active	dynamic	lead	simplify
aggressive	effective	listen	skill
agreement	efficiency	manage	solve
analyze	eliminate	monitor	streamline
assertive	energetic	motivate	strengthen
attitude	enthusiastic	participate	success
capable	establish	perform	synergy
careful	evaluate	persuade	systematic
common sense	excel	potential	tactful
conceive	excellence	precise	thorough
concurrence	expand	pride	train
conduct	expedite	produce	trim
conscientious	focus	professional	urgency
control	generate	proficiency	vital
develop	guide	provide	win
diplomatic	implement	recommend	

What do you do with this list? Incorporate the words into your everyday speech so that they flow naturally.

As you move through your job search, keep a list of ten of the words in your wallet or purse. Take them out frequently during the early phase of your search and construct sentences about yourself. Use one word per sentence and make it sound good.

After you incorporate the first ten into your vocabulary, add ten more. Keep it up until the entire list is part of your internal wiring. You and others will be amazed at the change in your speech and attitude and how quickly you begin to get offers.

Perfect Your Interview Delivery Techniques

You might not consider yourself an actor, but when you interview, you'll either wind up as the star in the job of your choice or an out-on-the-street extra. If you would star, you'd better be prepared. Here are proven techniques I've seen work over nearly three decades in the human relations and placement fields.

Identify and write down three or four typical problems you face in your current job. Break each issue down into basic components:

- *Nature of the Problem.* What is the solution? Is it typical or unusual? Was it a catastrophe? If it was the latter, be careful of pointing the finger of blame.
- *Relevant Background Information.* What parts of your background or education were useful in confronting the problem?
- *Key Qualities Leading to a Solution.* What professional skills and personal behavior helped solve the problem?
- *Specific Elements of the Solution.* How did the problem successfully turn out? (If it didn't, don't use it.)
- *Net Gain to Your Employer.* How did your company benefit? Quantify the solution in terms of money earned, money or time saved.
- *Restate Your Role.* Were you a team member or the leader in this problem-solving equation?

Once you've analyzed the problems typical to your current position and your role in their solutions, memorize them. Then store them away, ready for use when the right question is asked.

In other words, you rehearse. No, you won't sound like a mindless bionic brain spewing out facts and figures, because you'll customize the answers to each specific situation. Follow the steps given here and the interviewer will never know you've used the system. He or she won't care either, especially if you're the one to help make that job requisition vanish from an overloaded desk.

People who interview well are better employees, too. Why? They have learned to interact on a job—to sell themselves and their ideas to others. They aren't enslaved because they know they can always take their skills elsewhere and find another, better job.

Programmed interviewing puts you in control. You learn and retain the kinds of positive interviewing skills that get people hired, promoted, and recruited for better opportunities elsewhere.

Here are the six most important steps you need to ensure your interview success:

1. *Scan the script.* Read the questions and answers to yourself once.

2. *Customize it to your target job.* Adjust the questions as needed to conform to the ones you are likely to be asked.

3. *Customize it to your character.* Modify the language to your own style of speech. (Just don't stray too far from the essence of the answer; each is carefully designed and tested to score the most points for you.)

4. *Record and replay.* Prepare a cassette for yourself containing the most difficult questions for you to answer, leaving spaces to read your answers aloud. You can stop the tape occasionally to rehearse a particular response, but it's important to simulate an interview where the dialogue continues, just like real life.

5. *Rehearse your delivery.* Play the cassette at least three times a week for the next two weeks, sitting in front of a full-length mirror. Make an interviewing "set" by using a table for a desk and adding other props. Pay close attention to your facial expressions, hand movements, and body language. Smile. Look the interviewer (you in the mirror) in the eye. Try not to speak with your hands. Lean forward to make a point.

6. *Repeat it until it rolls off your tongue.* Use your driving, riding, or walking time to listen to the cassette and answer the questions. You can just think the answer, but talking aloud to an imagined interviewer really rivets your attention. Listen to yourself answering the questions, and they will become an ingrained part of your memory files, ready to be retrieved as necessary.

Maintain your poise and you'll maintain control. You will face questions and situations designed to entrap an unwary candidate. Among the most challenging:

1. *Never say anything critical about former employers.* Always answer a question about your impressions of your current employer in the

affirmative. If you have to bite your tongue till it bleeds in your rehearsal, come up with an answer that is positive. There is a very strong feeling that people who complain about past employers are troublemakers and that could be an automatic rejection for your candidacy.

2. *Admire the achievements of the prospective employer.* Just do so only if the admiration is genuine, based on fact, and is used sparingly. Use the information acquired through your research at appropriate places in the conversation. Your grasp of the situation will impress the interviewer.

3. *Don't be afraid to say "I don't know."* But do amend it with "I'd like to think about it a minute," or "I'll have to check that out and get back to you." If it's a really important question, it will give you a valid reason for calling the interviewer back.

4. *Don't contradict, argue with, or interrupt the interviewer.* If asked for your business opinion give it honestly, but if you disagree, do so in respectful language. "I can see how you might feel that way, however. . . ." or "Perhaps. . . .", "Maybe. . . .", "I could be wrong, but. . . ."

5. *Listen to the question that was asked and answer it.* If you don't understand it, ask for a clarification. "I'm not sure I understood the question. Do you mean . . . ?"

6. *Anytime you get flustered in an interview, ask a question.* This gives you time to think and gain some control. Whoever is asking the question becomes the party in control.

7. *Don't permit salary issues to come up too early.* If you seem too interested in the benefits, you'll soon be out of contention. If you agree to a lower figure early on, it's difficult to increase it later. If salary comes up prematurely, ask what they had in mind for the position. Then use lines like "We're in the same ballpark, but I'm really interested now in the job and its specifics. It will be easier to evaluate my salary needs when I know more about the job."

Twenty Knockout Questions

I could give you hundreds of questions you might be asked during the interview. Since you're already an experienced candidate, I've listed only some of the most tricky ones.

Personal Questions

Although personal questions are the easiest to answer, they are often the most emotionally charged. Rehearsing your answers to personal questions is particularly important, because what you convey is as crucial as what you say. While most of these and similar questions have only marginal value in determining ultimate qualifications, you have to get past them before you move onto real business. They can be the questions that knock you out before the second round even begins.

1. How much personal time do you spend with your family?

Be careful to project a balanced attitude here. This subject can be touchy. You may be dealing with an interviewer who lives by the credo, "Work is not the only way to make a living; it's the way to make a life." Or, you may be talking to one who recognizes the importance of a family. Before you answer, check out the situation. Do you see family photos, desk accessories made by children, or other warm, human touches? Customize your basic, generic answer as needed.

> "I suppose I spend an average amount with them. My family is important to me. My great relationship with them gives me the best reason in the world to succeed in my career. In that way, they are an inspiration. I have a responsibility to my job as well as to my family, since I've made a strong commitment to both. I like to be there for them when they need me, but they also understand and accept the commitment I have made to my work. So I spend my time accordingly."

2. Have you any chronic health problems we should consider?

If not, then simply answer no. The question is illegal, and the interviewer is asking for your opinion. The only time you should answer this question positively is if you do have a condition that will become evident in a preemployment physical, such as diabetes. In that case you might answer:

> "Nothing that would interfere with my work performance. I have had diabetes for 20 years, but I control it very successfully and unobtrusively. It has never been an issue in my work; and aside

from my family, only my doctor knows. It isn't a secret—it just has nothing to do with performing the job."

Character Questions

Be careful! Character is the most subjective area of all. The interviewer will try to take a reading of your character with the type of questions that follow. Rehearse this part of the script especially well so you don't flub your lines and reveal any quirks that might make the interviewer call "Cut!"

3. Do you consider yourself to be a smart person?

"Yes. That means I'm smart enough to know my opinion is biased. The kind of intelligence required on the job isn't always measured by an IQ test. Only through coping with different situations and interacting with other people can intelligence truly be judged. By these criteria, I'm above average in intelligence. When it comes to working with people, solving business problems, and making decisions—especially those related to the job—I'm as good or better than anyone else. There are many things I don't know, but I can learn. In that way, a smart person is the one who asks questions, listens carefully, and realizes nobody knows everything."

4. How important is job security to you?

"Security is a basic need, but I know that there are no guarantees in life. The only true job security comes from making a meaningful contribution to my employer. If I know my job will be around for as long as I excel at it, I am able to concentrate on my work and remain focused. The best environment is one where employer and employee form a partnership for their mutual benefit. The first priority of any job is the work itself. Everything else is secondary. As long as I find myself challenged by my work and am respected by those around me, I'm confident that I'll be able to continue getting the work done properly, always meeting or exceeding expectations."

5. What are the reasons for your success?

"I always give a hundred percent. Some people try to prove themselves to someone else, but I think sometimes it's better to prove to yourself that you can succeed. No one is a better judge of your success than you, and you know what you can do. When I do a job well, it gives me personal satisfaction that carries over into everything I do.

Although I work very hard, I find that I get along with all sorts of people. By respecting everyone as an individual as you advance in responsibility, you not only make a good impression but you also gain the respect of others.

Paying attention to details is also important. I usually like to recheck everything I do, just in case I missed something the first time. I also find it beneficial to at least review any work that has my name on it, even if completed by a secretary or someone else in my department. Proper delegation requires some supervision.

Eventually, hard work, respect for others, and attention to detail pay off, and they make the job more enjoyable and challenging."

6. How do you show interest in your coworkers?

"By keeping my eyes and ears open. I try to be sensitive to those around me. If someone behaves in a way that is different from what I expect, I ask myself, "Why? Are there problems that have caused this person to behave differently?"

On a day-to-day basis, I try to remember the little things that are important to the people around me. I follow up and ask them how things are going without becoming overbearing. Work teams often become like a family, and it's important to remember that coworkers need to be appreciated, liked, and respected.

If I am the supervisor in the relationship, I usually call a quick, closed-door conference to see if there's something that can be done before a possible problem becomes a probable one."

7. Do you have a competitive nature?

"Yes. A competitive nature is necessary to be successful in a corporate environment. But competitiveness doesn't mean vying with my coworkers for recognition, raises, or promotions. If I do my work well and always give my best effort, the rewards will come. I've found that's the only real way to succeed.

But I do compete with myself. I'm always trying to break my own record—to do something better or faster than I did it the last time. I'm especially competitive when it comes to improving my company's product or service.

There's so much potential for accomplishment when you're part of a vibrant company like this one."

Initiative and Creativity Questions

These questions focus on *what* and *why*. For interviewing purposes, concentrate on the parts of former jobs that you improved. Then work backwards.

Begin with what you did, then why. Next, tie these improvements into the target job. You'll be surprised how easy this is since initiative and creativity are part of the highly transferable job skills discussed earlier. I've left blanks in the script so you can tailor the answers to your own experience.

8. What do you do when you have difficulty solving a problem?

"One thing I don't do is ignore it and hope it will go away. I'm not afraid to ask questions or look for answers myself. There is a solution to every problem. Sometimes it just takes creative investigation. I'm a problem solver by nature. Nothing puzzles me for long. If it does, I just keep working until I find a solution."

9. What are the most boring and the most interesting jobs you've ever had?

"I haven't found any of the work in my adult career 'boring.' I've always been too busy to be bored!

Perhaps, as a teenager, you could say I wasn't very excited about some of the part-time work available. But I always found something positive about every job. When I was behind the counter at a fast-food store selling one thousand hamburgers daily, the routine was eased by all the different people I met. There has been something interesting, something that held my attention about every job I've held, or I don't think I would have taken the job in the first place.

My most interesting job to date has been _____, because of _____. I received particularly favorable performance reviews in that job, but I've had excellent ratings in all my work. When I make a commitment to a job, I give it all I've got."

10. Is there a lot of pressure in your current job? How do you cope with it?

"There is pressure in every job. In my present job, the pressure is usually associated with production deadlines or special projects. Experience has taught me how to cope with pressure.

All jobs have more demands at some times than others. The key is to manage your time and prioritize the work so you're ready for anything. When I work out the details and set the schedule in advance, I see that any big job can be broken down into many smaller jobs. Taken one at a time, any task can be mastered. I respond to pressure; I don't react to it. After analyzing the components of the project, I take a few steps back so I can see the big picture. This approach has seen me through many a tough situation with results that exceeded what anyone imagined— except perhaps me."

11. How do you go about making important decisions?

"I evaluate my options, laying them all out in front of me. I find it helps to write down briefly what my alternatives are, so I can examine them objectively. Then I rely on past experience, company policies and—in part—intuition to guide me to a decision. I look at each situation individually and weigh possible outcomes before making a choice.

If it's a big decision that has no precedent, I get input from the staff who will be affected by it as well as my superiors who will be called upon to explain my decision."

Questions About Management Ability

You're an MBA. That stands for Most Believable Applicant. Since the ability to manage depends on substantial personal contact, it's virtually impossible for your skill to be measured. The closest an interviewer can get is to find out where you learned to apply basic principles.

If you've never been a job manager, think about other positions where you've supervised others. Even charity fund-raising and community service projects can be effectively woven into the script. Managing a dozen volunteers can be the equivalent of directing a cast of hundreds.

Your local public library stocks numerous books and periodicals on management. A few of the most current ones are all you need to pick up theory, the latest buzzwords, or an interesting case study.

12. As a department manager, how would you establish staff rapport?

"First, I would want to know as much about each individual as I could, professionally as well as personally. Every employee is an individual and cannot be evaluated solely by arbitrary standards. Independent judgment is the major part of every manager's job, and there can be several right ways to approach something.

By reviewing each individual's position and work record, I would gain insight about his or her strong points and weaknesses. Similarly, by meeting with each person on a one-to-one basis and making myself open to candid dialogue, the stage would be set for a healthy working relationship.

Too many supervisor-subordinate relations are like two monologues rather than one dialogue. This is a management problem and a manager's responsibility to solve. In a word, I'd start by listening."

13. What do your subordinates think are your strengths? Your weaknesses?

"The people who have worked for me will tell you I am fair and I have a balanced approach to managing that considers both the business and people side of every issue. They know I don't make decisions in haste that everyone will repent at leisure. And, working for me usually means being on a winning team, where the coach asks everyone to give 110 percent. I ask a lot, but they love it.

What might be perceived by some as "weakness" are really my strengths. I expect a lot from my staff, but no more than I expect from myself. I look for and reward people who show initiative and creativity. People I've supervised will say that they worked harder in my department than in any other job. They'll also tell you they enjoyed it more because they were accomplishing more."

14. What steps would you take to terminate an employee who is not performing adequately?

"First, I'd make sure I followed all applicable company rules and procedures and any laws that govern the given situation.

People should have at least one warning and a chance to improve their performance. I would counsel them confidentially and give a written warning covering a specific period of time, along with clear guidelines for improvement. Then I would watch carefully and be sure to acknowledge and praise the employee for a sincere effort to remedy the situation.

However, if counseling and warning fail to produce results, I would not hesitate to terminate the employee. Firing is probably the hardest thing a manager does, because you come to know your employees as people. But, when someone who is notified that his or her work is below acceptable standards won't take steps to save his or her own job, the manager must protect the company. Again, I would make sure my actions were properly documented and that justifiable cause for termination was shown."

15. What plan of action do you take when facing a problem?

"Before I act, I think. I try to distance myself from the problem so that I can look at it objectively and analyze all sides. Sometimes I even write it down to see it more clearly.

When I've reached a decision, I present my planned solution to the people affected by it or those who must carry it out. I get their input, add any suggestions that are appropriate, and then we implement the plan. I believe in immediate but realistic solutions to problems, not ignoring them."

Career Objective Questions

Your career objective should vary depending on the target job. That's why in Chapter 6 I advised not to state your objective on your resume and to be careful in what you write on your application form. The job-search research you've been doing will help you customize your answers.

16. Why do you want this job?

"Because of the challenge and the opportunities at _____.
I'm well qualified for it, and this is exactly the kind of [competitive/creative/progressive/technically-oriented—*use an adjective appropriate to the company and the type of work*] atmosphere I've been looking for. My career goal is _____ and this job would allow me to develop my potential further while actively participating in that kind of work.

I've been offered a number of other opportunities, but after evaluating those jobs and companies, I decided not to make a move. Making a job change is a major decision, a long-term commitment that I take very seriously.

After researching the history and future plans of _____, meeting people who work here, and seeing the kinds of jobs there are to be done, it seems like a perfect fit!"

17. When do you expect a promotion?

"I would like my career to continue progressing as well as it has in the past. But I'm a realist. I know promotions aren't given, they're earned. When I've mastered my present position, improved it with my ideas, prepared myself to take on new responsibilities, and trained someone to take over my job, I'll be ready for a promotion."

Questions About the Target Job

If you've done your "phonework," you should have a basis for answering these questions. Suitability for a job is really just specialized use of certain learned information and practical skills. Almost everything we do on the job (even a highly skilled one) is common sense.

To match your skills to the target job and sell the interviewer on your suitability for it, do your job research; then combine your unique background experience and qualifications with the interview skills you've learned here.

18. What do you know about our company?

In your job-search research single out two or three positive facts about the company, such as growth in recent years, increasing market share, and innovative breakthroughs. Print these facts neatly on cue cards—3-by-5-inch index cards—for rehearsing your script. Just don't take your cue cards into the interview. You might also want to include any other information you picked up during your research, such as:

> "Most importantly, I've heard that _____ offers a challenging work environment that expects a great deal from people and gives them the opportunity to realize their potential. That's what I look for in an employer—an active, creative environment where I am limited only by my capabilities, and where positive results are acknowledged."

19. What specific ways can our company benefit from hiring you?

> "It will be getting someone whose skills and training most closely match the job requirements. Further, it will be getting the benefit of my experience at _____ and _____ .
>
> My background relates directly to the position being considered and is a primary reason why it will take me less time to produce than someone who hasn't had as much direct experience.
>
> Furthermore, I'm dedicated and learn quickly. I try always to excel at what I do, so when you hire me, there's little risk you'll be interviewing for the job again soon."

20. How do you manage to interview while still employed; may we contact your present employer?

> "I'm using personal time I've earned, since I rarely take sick leave. I arrange my interview schedule so that I am not away from my job more than one day at a time.

Sometimes it means working extra hours, but I take my responsibilities seriously. No one has to cover for me. In addition, I check in through the day for messages and to see if any situations need attention. I've developed a system for the work flow. As a result, no order sits on my desk, and nothing is delayed in my absence. Employees do themselves and their employees a disservice by getting themselves overloaded or in a position where they are the only ones who can do a job. If you take care of the little things, the big ones take care of themselves. A little organization, self-discipline, and prioritizing go a long way."

If you do NOT want your present employer contacted, say:

"As far as my employer goes, I have not yet told him. So please let me know before you contact anyone there. Once there's a firm offer on the table or you've narrowed the field to only a few candidates, the information I've given can be verified.

My boss deserves the courtesy of hearing I'm leaving from me. He'll be upset, but I'll assure him everything will be done to ensure the most efficient transfer of my duties."

If your employer knows you are interviewing and would give you a good reference, say:

"Yes, my employer knows I am interviewing, and understands the reason. We've had a good working relationship for the past _____ years. But now I've reached the highest level possible there, and I've trained people to assume my duties.

My boss regrets not being able to offer more at this time and understands that I'm not working to my full potential. We're parting on good terms."

Getting the Leading Edge

Listening and questioning properly is the way to win the interview and get the job. For the first minutes of the interview, you've been observing and determining how to proceed. Then you've been asked impossible questions and delivered inspirational answers.

As you proceed, questions you ask the interviewer demonstrate your interest in the job. They also give you the opportunity to lead the interviewer into your strongest areas.

Your questions and the interviewer's answers shouldn't exceed more than ten percent of the interview time. Since you don't know how long the interview will last, just ask a question after you have answered about nine of them. No—don't write tally marks on your note pad. Just make notes of what you might like to ask.

Asking questions is an important part of pacing and leading the interview. Questioning must be done naturally at optimum times and in a nonthreatening manner. No question should be asked unless the answer will make you appear interested, intelligent, and qualified.

The average applicant talks about 85 percent of the time during an interview. That's why average applicants rarely get hired. Applicants who get hired zip their lips 50 percent of the time. This indicator of whether an offer will be extended is one of the most accurate, and you can control it.

Use questions as zippers to help you. Don't ask personal, controversial, or negative questions of any kind.

Questions With a Favorable Impact

"How many employees does the company have?"
"What are the company's plans for expansion?"
"How many employees does the department have?"
"Does the department work separately from other departments?"
"Are the department's functions important to senior management?"
"What is the supervisor's management style?"
"To whom does the supervisor report?"
"Are you ready and able to hire now?"
"How long will it take to make a hiring decision?"
"What does the company consider the five most important duties of the position?"
"What do you expect the employee you hire to accomplish?"

Using Tie-Downs

The basic purpose of the questions you've been asking is to *lead* the interviewer along. Next comes the use of tie-downs, phrases used in questions designed to elicit an affirmative response.

The Most Common Tie-Down Phrases

"Aren't [I/you/we/they]?"
"Can't [I/he/she/you/we/they/it]?"
"Doesn't [he/she/it]?"
"Don't [I/you/we/they]?"
"Hasn't [he/she/it]?"

"Haven't [I/you/we/they]?"
"Isn't [he/she/it]?"
"Isn't that right?"
"Shouldn't [I/he/she/you/we/they/it]?"
"Wasn't [I/he/she/it]?"
"Weren't [you/we/they]?"
"Won't [I/he/she/you/we/they/it]?"
"Wouldn't [I/he/she/you/we/they/it]?"

Specific Tie-Downs

There are four kinds of tie-downs. Vary your dialogue with them, so you don't appear overbearing. With each agreement you obtain from the interviewer, you have scored one more minor yes leading to that major yes—the offer.

The best way to learn tie-down questioning techniques is the same way you rehearse your script for the interview. You write down all the tie-downs you can use during the interview, then read them into a tape recorder and play them back once or twice a day—every day—to implant them into your subconscious. They'll pop out automatically when you need them.

1. Standard tie-downs are used at the end of the question.

"My qualifications appear to fit the position you have open, don't they?"
"Diversified Investments really has a lot to offer someone with my experience, doesn't it?"
"It looks as if we'll be able to eliminate the problem, don't you agree?"

2. Inverted tie-downs are used at the beginning of a question.

"Isn't it an excellent position for someone with my background?"
"Don't you think we'll work together well?"
"Wouldn't you like to see how I can be of assistance?"

3. Internal tie-downs are used in the middle of a compound question.

"Since the entire data processing staff agrees, shouldn't we discuss when I can start work?"

"When the budget is approved, won't it expedite production to have someone who knows the project?"

"Now that we've had the opportunity to meet, wouldn't it be great to work together?"

4. Tag-on tie-downs are used after a statement of fact.

A slight pause, then emphasis on the tie-down improves its effect.

"My experience will benefit Allied Products, won't it?"

"You've really spent a lot of time and money to get the right person, haven't you?"

"This problem can be corrected easily, can't it?"

After you've rehearsed tie-downs for about a week, they will come naturally to you. You can begin your dialogue with a general question such as, "National Manufacturing leads the market with this product, *doesn't it?*" Then hone in for the win with questions such as, *"Wouldn't it* be interesting to work for a supervisor like that?" or "Now that the budget has been approved, *isn't it* essential to get started immediately?" And finally, *"Shouldn't I* give notice?"

Remember: overuse of questions can be grating. It makes you sound as if you are auditioning for a game show rather than starring in a "screen test." For best results, use sparingly, like fine spices to flavor your interview.

Closing the Interview

After about forty-five minutes to an hour of interviewing (no more) you should be on your way. An important clue is when you hear a positive comment such as, "This is the kind of experience we need."

When you feel the timing is right, lean slightly forward in your chair, smile, look the interviewer in the eye and say in a warm, declarative tone something like:

"My background fits the position well."

"We have a good match here."

"This looks like a long-term situation."

"I'm excited about the position."

"Everything looks good."

You're nearly through the interview. Still there are several more minefields capable of exploding. Before the interview concludes, there are a number of dos and don'ts to remember.

First Interview Exit Dos

- If the offer is extended during the first interview (unusual, but possible for upper-level candidates), show decisiveness. React with enthusiasm. Then sleep on it. If this is not possible, accept with grace, so you're in control; you can always change your mind later on.
- Review the job requirements with the interviewer, and relate, point by point, how they match up with your qualifications.
- Determine if this is the *only* interview. If it is, you must ask for the job in a positive and enthusiastic fashion. Ask about the time frame and end on a high note: "I really like the sound of this opportunity. Since you will be making a decision by the twentieth, what must I do in the meantime to ensure that I get the job?" *Note:* This is the only time in which you should even remotely appear to be asking for the job.
- If a second round of interviews is planned, check on their timing. Be firm and upfront about what you want: "Is this a good time to schedule the next interview?" If you don't ask, you may not get it.
- Be a winning contender. A good closing question is: "Until I hear from you again, what are the primary aspects of the job I should be considering?"
- Stand up and follow through with the Magic Four Goodbye:
  1. A smile.
  2. Direct eye contact.
  3. The words "It sounds like a fine opportunity. I look forward to hearing from you."
  4. A firm but gentle handshake.

Then leave without asking for the job. Is there really any doubt as to why you're there? This is closing with class.

First Interview Exit Don'ts

- Don't discuss salary, vacation, or benefits until the offer is extended. It makes you look as if you have money on the mind instead of selling yourself on your merits.
- Don't press for an early decision. You may ask "When will I know your decision?" Just don't press it. Forcing the issue may

force you out of candidacy. Don't use "other offers I'm considering" if none exist. It can annoy the interviewer and force you into negotiating from a position of weakness.

- Don't show discouragement. It shows a lack of self-esteem. Usually a job offer is not extended on the spot. Leave with a golden glow and the reflection you cast will follow you into the appropriate offer.
- Don't ask the interviewer to evaluate your performance. Again, this puts him or her in an awkward spot (certainly not the way you want the interview to conclude).

Chapter 9

Salary, Follow-Up, and Second Interviews

Although salary questions are usually brought up after you move into serious contention for a position, you must avoid painting yourself into a corner on the job application. When you fill it out, where it asks for salary requirements, write "open." If the form specifically advises that "open" is not an acceptable answer, write "negotiable" or "competitive."

Salary Requirements

The later into the interview the salary question arises, the better. Many times salary discussions are deferred to the second interview. You'll know the moment to discuss money has arrived in one of two ways:

1. The interviewer will begin to advance the offer by comments such as, "You could make a real contribution here" or "How do you think you'd like working here?"
2. You push the issue yourself, when it feels right, with tie-downs like, "With my background and knowledge, I feel I could make an important contribution, don't you?" or "It seems like we've got a great match, don't you think?" or "How do you think I would fit in here?"

Be Prepared With Facts

Make sure you have all the facts in hand. Clarify all your responsibilities and check out what salary range is realistic. There are several ways to get this information.

- See if the personnel office will provide you salary ranges for positions above and below you. Do this as an anonymous call-in.
- See information from the Bureau of Labor Statistics in Washington, D.C. They have statistics on hundreds of job titles. Allow for the fact that they may be slightly out of date.
- Check out your state employment offices for similar information.
- Get to know a friendly headhunter. He or she deals with such issues daily in the real world.
- Check your local library for back issues of *The National Business Employment Weekly*, which regularly runs salary surveys.

Before doing *any* negotiating, make sure the employer is going to extend an offer. If the company isn't sure about you, premature financial discussions may turn them off quickly. In any case, once you get into the negotiating posture, there can be no going back.

Salary Negotiating Techniques

Employers like bargains but are suspicious of too good a deal. They expect seekers to want more.

Set optimistic goals. Sell quality rather than lower starting rate. If you want to change jobs for financial reasons, you should be looking for at least a 20 percent increase in net annual take-home pay. A simple formula to follow: Determine your dream salary. Define your basic "reality" salary. Then negotiate for the midpoint range.

When the interviewer initially asks what numbers you are looking for, don't give them any unless they are on the high end. Or use phrases like "I expect a salary commensurate with my expenses and the job's responsibilities. No doubt the company has established a salary range. What do you have in mind?"

If you get wedged into a box and are specifically asked what you are paid, you can respond to the effect, "Currently I earn x, although my present job and the position you have here are substantially different."

You can also add on to your job figures such benefits as medical and dental plans. These are particularly beneficial if you are substantially underpaid in your present job. For many people, benefits can add 20 percent to 35 percent onto the totals of their current salaries and are honest figures that can stand scrutiny. Sit down with pencil and paper and add up the worth of pay in lieu of profit sharing, bonuses, pension plans, stock purchase plans and other fringes. Don't forget the value of a company car, tuition reimbursement, and even subsidized meals in the employee cafeteria.

Then you can answer truthfully, "My base salary is $48,000. With overtime, end-of-year bonus, company-matched savings plans, pension, and profit sharing, I earn $60,000 excluding complete medical insurance coverage."

Answering Salary Questions

Here is where you must be at your sharpest. Peg your value too high, and you're noncompetitive; ask for a lower salary "to get in the door," and you demean your worth.

[*Question: What salary are you worth?*]

"An employee's worth is measured by his or her contribution to an employer. I expect to contribute and to be paid a salary commensurate with that contribution. I know you'll be fair— otherwise I wouldn't accept or stay.

"Once hired, my first priority is to do the job I'm being paid to do. And, if I perform well, I expect to advance accordingly. However, money is not foremost in my mind. Too much concern about the paycheck can lead to a poor attitude and result in a poor job. As long as I focus on doing the best job possible, I doubt I'll have anything to worry about."

[*Question: Do you expect to be rewarded for work you consider to be well done?*]

"Not necessarily. In the world of work, the rewards don't always follow the effort.

"Like most people, I want to have my income increase. But, as a mature person, I realize that there are other considerations, too. Recognition in the form of monetary reward is always gratifying, but it can be equally fulfilling to meet a challenge with success and see the results of your efforts on the job. That's a personal type of reward no amount of money can buy.

"I've always looked upon making a living as only one part of making a life. The feeling I get when my extra effort results in excellence is the real reward. If others don't recognize my achievements, there's always the next project."

[*Question: What would you like to be earning two/five/ten years from now?*]

"At any point in my career, I'd like my salary to keep pace with inflation and be competitive with what similar positions pay.

"However, I don't see myself as an 'average' employee. I always strive for excellence and never settle for anything less than above average. So, logically, my income should reflect that.

"As long as my paycheck is an investment by the company that earns a return, the higher the rate of return the more it should invest. If I'm not performing at any time, I shouldn't be here. I have no illusions about employment as a value-for-value relationship."

[Question: What is your salary history?]

"I'd be happy to give you specific numbers and percentages of increase from year to year, but I'm not able to recite them from memory now. Salary just isn't as important to me as opportunity.

"At every salary review, I received merit increases. My salary has always been a reflection of my work progress and contribution to my employer's success. Anything less than that doesn't work for long."

If you are pressed, you can reiterate something to the effect that:

"I'll be glad to give you exact information, but I need to figure it out at home."

Very likely the interviewer will not ask you to do that. If he or she does, agree, but wait until you're asked a second time. If and when finally pressed to reveal your salary, be sure to state:

"Despite my significant contribution, I received the same pay increases as some lesser-qualified employees. Over the long haul, I want to be in a company where my individual achievements may be recognized and rewarded. Is that something I can expect at Johnson Manufacturing?"

[Question: Have you ever been turned down for a salary increase?]

"I've never had to ask for a raise. My performance evaluations were always positive, and my salary reviews consistently resulted in increases. In some years, the increases were lower than in others due to overall financial conditions. But have I ever been refused a raise because of inadequate performance? No."

[Question: Do you have any outside income?]

This is none of their business and shouldn't even be considered when determining your suitability for the job. Your spouse's income is not yours, so your answer should be no. They don't need to know that you receive a nice monthly check from a trust fund set up by a grandparent. Child support payments are income you receive on behalf of your children, not yourself. So unless you have another job or income from a business on the side, your answer is always no. Of course, if you're in the National Guard or any of the military reserves, do explain. Since most employers support these, consenting to a little invasion of privacy might advance you directly from job-seeking maneuvers onto the employment battlefield. If you do derive additional income from part-time or self-employment, plan your response carefully. Will the interviewer perceive your moonlighting as an interference with the target job? Consider this sample answer:

> "I occasionally work part time in the evenings or on weekends as a [bartender/private duty nurse/aerobics instructor], but I have no other professional commitment on a regular basis. I have the right of refusal, and the people I work with understand my priorities. I never let fill-in work interfere with my primary job. It's just been a source of extra income from time to time.

> **[Question: How far can you lower your salary expectations to be in line with our rate for the position?]**

> "It would be difficult to accept much less than my present salary. I don't know too many people who want or can afford to lower their standard of living.
> "However, if you can tell me when my salary would increase and to what level, based on my satisfactory performance, I would consider a temporary cut."

Additional Benefits and How to Obtain Them

Today's top executives usually participate in short-term incentive programs. Bonus payments play a major role in executive compensation. This type of income incentive is always at risk, because you must meet or exceed specific goals before you get the rewards.

In the late 1980s the average executive compensation package was 40 percent base salary, 20 percent short-term incentives, 20 percent long-term incentives, 15 percent benefits, and 5 percent perquisites. Within those numbers is a big area for negotiation. So what you can get through base salary may be more than offset in other benefits.

Once you are past the base salary discussions, it's time to tackle future remuneration. You might say something such as, "We're getting close on the salary. Now let's focus on the future."

The basic precept is to ask. If you don't, you won't get it. Naturally, the higher you go in executive management, the more realistic your opportunity to secure these prizes.

Typical Future Financial Incentives

- Automobile
- Automobile maintenance and travel reimbursement
- Bonuses and other monetary incentives
- Competitive range of group insurance coverages
- Extended vacations, sick leave, and personal time
- Legal services
- Liberal profit sharing
- Long-term disability and other income security insurance
- Pension and other retirement plans
- Pre-employment signing bonus
- Relocation assistance including moving expenses
- Salary increase and additional bonus within six months
- Semi-annual merit increases
- Subsidized stock options

Negotiating the Offer

Negotiating a salary and benefits package is much like negotiating a loan. The more you look like you need it, the less likely you are to get it.

Let the two precepts of the art of negotiating work for you:

1. "The one who does the most talking ends up giving away the store."
2. "The less you sweat, the more you get."

When you receive an offer, regardless of how good it sounds, never accept on the spot. Be positive, exclaim how enthusiastic you are about the offer, and request time to think it over—anything from overnight to a couple of extra days. Then discuss it with your spouse or significant other. During this standard cooling-off period, talk to people whose advice you trust. Weigh their objective points of view with your gut feelings.

Also during this period, you should weigh salary, future earnings, overall career prospects, commute, and lifestyle. Ask yourself the following questions:

- Do you like the work?
- Do you have a realistic shot at success?
- Are the title and responsibilities an upward move for you?
- Are the atmosphere and "corporate culture" to your liking?
- Can you get along with your superior and immediate work group?
- Is the salary and compensation package the best you can get?

Once you accept the job, do it verbally. Then get it in writing. Verbal offers can be withdrawn for a variety of reasons, and you won't have a leg to stand on.

How to Leverage the Compensation Package Upward

While you're assessing your future with the company that made you the offer, you can use the time to leverage the opportunity. If you've been interviewing regularly (and I assume by this time you've been doing so), you can take your newfound strength to other target companies. Call and tell them you've received a job offer from one of their competitors: "I didn't want to make a final decision without the opportunity to speak with you again. Can we schedule a meeting in the next couple of days?"

If you've been a prime candidate at another company, now you'll look even better. After all, we want most what we cannot have. You're calling the shots now with other companies whose offers you may still be awaiting.

While you are negotiating with the company that looks best (assuming you get multiple offers), you should be absolutely enthusiastic about everything but the financial part. Be totally outgoing in your excitement about the job, your future boss, the company, and the great opportunity presented to you. Then see how much more you can negotiate for. Once you accept, that opportunity vanishes.

Follow Up the Interview to Best Advantage

Although I've discussed salary negotiations and closing the offer, in fact, they very seldom come after the first interview. There is usually a lag and you await that second confirming interview.

While you wait, there's much you can do. After all, out of sight, out of mind. How can you keep your candidacy alive while the interviewer sees other candidates? Correspondence, telephone calls, and networking keep you in front of the interviewer while you're also out getting offers elsewhere.

Image the Interview

This step is a major reason for leaving time between interviews. You've got to get to a quiet place—even if it's only your car—and replay the interview in your head.

You must be your own toughest critic, with a no-holds-barred self-critique. Try to see yourself and the interviewer interacting. Did you assess the interviewer's style accurately, align with him or her, pace, and lead? Did the interviewer smile and nod his or her head a lot? Did you sense positive reinforcement?

Answer the following questions:

- Did I make a positive first impression with the Magic Four Hello? (See Chapter 8.)
- Did the interviewer and I have rapport?
- Did I use tie-downs to secure agreement?
- Did I access my action vocabulary and success phrases?
- Did I thank the interviewer?
- Did my closing statement lead into the next meeting?
- What did I do wrong?

After mentally reviewing your performance, write down the facts. What did you learn about the job and the company? Note names of individuals, their titles, details about the organization, and anything else you can use for your follow-up letters and phone calls, second interviews, and negotiations.

As soon as possible, record all the facts about the company, the position, and your performance on an "interviewer evaluation form." In the meantime, your interviewer will be filling out his or her own. Exhibit 9-1 is a sample you can use, and Exhibit 9-2 is a sample follow-up plan.

Create the Best Follow-Up Letter

I covered the basics of letter appearance in Chapter 6, but just for review, the letter should:

- Be word processed on a computer with a good quality printer or on an electronic typewriter with a carbon ribbon.

Exhibit 9-1.   Interview evaluation form.

Interview day, date, and time: _____

Name of company: _____

Address: _____

Phone: _____

Name of interviewer: _____

Title: _____ Phone: _____

Personal characteristics of interviewer: _____

_____

Title of positions(s) available: _____

Duties: _____

_____

Reports to: [Name] _____ [Title] _____

Number of people supervised: _____

Salary range: _____

Bonus or other benefits: _____

_____

Salary review period: _____

Next career step: _____

Company information learned during interview: _____

_____

My qualifications for position include: _____

_____

Any weaknesses I have relating to position: _____

_____

Job assets: _____

Job liabilities: _____

Review of my interview performance: _____

_____

_____

_____

Interviewer seemed most impressed by my: _____

_____

Weakest areas during interview were: _____

_____

_____

Exhibit 9-2. Follow-up plan.

Follow-up letters (name and date sent):

1. _____ Date: _____

2. _____ Date: _____

3. _____ Date: _____

Follow-up phone calls (name and date):

1. _____ Date: _____

Nature of discussion: _____

_____

2. _____ Date: _____

Nature of discussion: _____

_____

Other follow-up (internal referrals and references):

1. _____ Date: _____

2. _____ Date: _____

Plan of action and questions to ask in next interview: _____

_____

_____

- Be written on high-quality personal letterhead, with no errors or erasures.
- Be no longer than one page.
- Be fully addressed with no abbreviations, misspellings, or inaccuracies.
- Contain the middle initial and title of the interviewer. (Double-check exact title and spellings.)
- Be brief, enthusiastic, and to the point.

You only have a small amount of space, so use it to your best advantage. Accentuate your assets and accomplishments, and convincingly describe how you can benefit the employer. Include the properly spelled names of people you met and buzzwords familiar to the interviewer. End with words similar to the Magic Four Goodbye (see Chapter 8), requesting a reply as soon as possible.

You can adapt the following seven components of a letter to the target job and personality of the interviewer.

1. *Address line*. The full company name, full address (no abbreviations), full name of the interviewer, and his or her full title. These make you look thorough and professional.

2. *Subject line*. This zeroes in on the contents and dresses up the letter.

> Re: Interview for the Position of (title) on (date)

3. *Greeting*. "Miss" or "Mrs." should not be used unless you know the interviewer does so. First names are out of the question, even if they were used during the interview.

> "Dear Mr./Ms. _____"

4. *Opening*. Begin on a gracious note. Try to include all who were present at the interview.

> "It was a pleasure meeting with you last _____ to discuss the opening in _____ with Company X."

> "I appreciated meeting with _____ and yourself in your office on _____ to discuss the _____ position with Company X."

> "Thanks again for taking the time to see me regarding the opening in the _____ department."

5. *Body*. Comment on or add to something discussed during your interview in the body of the letter. Choosing a topic that allows you to emphasize directly or implicitly your qualifications will keep your follow-up from being just another routine thank-you.

> "From our discussion and the fine reputation of your organization, it appears that the _____ position would enable me to fully use my background in _____."

> "I was particularly impressed with the professionalism evident throughout my visit. Company X appears to have the kind of environment I have been seeking."

> "The atmosphere at Company X seems to strongly favor individual involvement, and I would undoubtedly be able to contribute significantly to its goals."

6. *Closing.* Your closing should display enthusiasm, and, if possible, put pressure on the prospective employer for a prompt, positive decision.

> "While I have been considering other situations, I have deferred a decision until I hear from you. Therefore, your prompt reply would be greatly appreciated."

> "It's an exciting opportunity. I look forward to hearing your decision soon."

> "The _____ position and Company X are exactly what I have been seeking, and I hope to hear from you within the next week."

7. *Salutation.*

> "Sincerely,"
> "Very truly yours,"
> "Best regards,"

You don't want the rosy impression you left with your interviewer to grow cold. Once written, get the letter in the mail immediately. It should arrive no later than three days after your interview. If you interviewed on a Monday or Tuesday, have it there by Wednesday or Thursday. Since Fridays and Mondays are overload times, letters that follow Wednesday or Thursday interviews should be timed for arrival the following Tuesday.

Another "Deep Breath" Phone Call

If you hear nothing after five days (which is normal), pick up the phone, take a deep breath, smile, and call. There are several reasons to call back:

▪ You have a more thorough answer to a question posed during the interview. For example:

> "You asked about the copy that I wrote for the infomercial on beauty care. I just saw the finished video on Channel 3 last night, and it very closely matched my script."

- You have an additional solution to a problem. "After we talked about your new sales incentive program, I began to think about the gain sharing plan at Ideal Industries. I'd like to put those ideas in writing and drop them off—say at 3:45 tomorrow?" Then, you can use the time generated in this extra "mini interview" to reiterate your interest.

- You want to check in by phone with any internal referral and friends you made during your research of the target employer. Tell them a few positive things about the interview. Inquire subtly if they've "heard anything." If they're receptive, ask them to "Put in a good word for me."

- Once you've finished with an interview, be sure to call the people you've given as references and tell them how your interview went. Doing this primes them so that when the interviewer does call to confirm a reference, they'll be ready. I discuss those well-chosen references in Chapter 10.

If you've been interviewed by other than a human resources representative, it may take a little more perseverance to get through. Here's a workable solution:

Enlist the executive secretary or assistant as your ally, not your adversary. A courteous, firm tone of voice works wonders. Don't play guessing games to get around the front desk. An executive always states his name. Only nobodies have no names. And don't ask nosy questions about the boss's schedule, hoping to catch him unguarded. A good secretary simply will not tell you. In any case, if you call very early (before 9:00 A.M.) or late (after 5:00 P.M.), you can often get through directly. If you speak to the secretary:

SECRETARY: Good morning, Mr. _____ office.

YOU: This is _____ calling. May I speak to him please?

SECRETARY: I'm sorry, he's stepped away from his desk/on another line/in a meeting. May I take a message?

YOU: Mr. _____ and I met last week regarding the _____ position.

SECRETARY: One minute, please.

The boss might very well have stepped away, be on another line, or in a meeting. More likely the secretary is checking to see if he wants to take the call or not. If not:

You: When would be a good time to call back? [*or*] I'll hold, please.

Since you have been direct and helpful, the secretary is very likely to return the courtesy. Also be polite and stubborn: you'll get the decision maker and a decision before long.

The Second Interview

The second interview is often equated with getting the job. Statistically, this is true nearly 60 percent of the time.

It is critical to recognize the differences between the two interviews. You're more self-assured. The initial fear of the unknown is gone. You know the job's parameters and have assessed your own feelings about it.

If your first interview took place in human resources, the next is very likely to be with your future boss and others in the department with the job opening. If it's a top-level position, you may meet with the board of directors or the executive committee. If you already made direct contact with the supervisor and your second interview is with human resources, then you've probably already won the job. The second interview then becomes a mere formality. Since the more likely scenario is that you'll be moving up the chain of command, it's important that you anticipate what comes next.

Generally, you'll have passed through personnel screening and are now working on your future supervisor (supervisor in this case means any functional hiring authority from the CEO on down). At this point, you must use every means at your disposal to understand what makes him or her tick.

Calling the Initial Interviewer

By now, you should have several acquaintances within the company. One especially strong ally may be your first interviewer. By now, he or she has a vested interest in you. The interviewer knows that if too many applicants become real candidates, the supervisor will delay in filling the job. That means one more bit of unfinished paperwork left lying on the interviewer's desk.

When you call the interviewer, first express your appreciation. Then lead into a discussion with something like, "From what I understand, I'll really be able to assist _____.
Is there anything else I should know?" Then listen hard and take

notes fast. The interviewer should be pleased to give you her impressions. Often, they are very incisive since she has access to personnel files. Before you end the conversation, ask if she thinks the supervisor would mind a direct call. Interpret her "No, I don't," as a suggestion that you do so.

Then call the supervisor. Say something like, "I'm looking forward to meeting you on _____. Before we get together, is there anything you'd like me to bring?" Ninety-nine times out of one hundred the supervisor will not be able to think that fast. On the remote chance that he does, evaluate whether it can adversely affect you. If so, say, "I'll check to see if I have it. If not, I'll bring what I can."

This is more than just a chance to confirm the next interview. It shows you in some detail where the supervisor's head is at and which tack you should take.

If arrangements call for you to be introduced to the supervisor by your first interviewer, so much the better, for two reasons: First, you should have time to talk to the interviewer before introductions are made, and you can gently press for additional information. Second, when you're introduced by someone else in the company, some positive transference takes place. The meeting will be off to a warm, friendly start.

What you talk about at the second interview depends on who's doing the interview. Generally the second interview is more directed. It takes one of two paths, and you should be prepared for both:

1. *The "Who Are You?" Interview.* If it's an executive committee or another person near the top, expect a relatively general interview where you discuss personal goals and objectives and those of the company. By now you should have developed a clearer profile of your interviewer and the target job.
2. *The "What Can You Do For Us?" Interview.* If the second interview is with your prospective supervisor, anticipate a direct, job-related session. Expect to discuss the specific contributions you can make. Be prepared to demonstrate exactly how your background, experience, and skills enable you to do the target job. It's a more objective approach, and you can be fully prepared.

Developing Your Technical Vocabulary

It's time to dust off the buzzwords we discussed in Chapter 8. Emphasize state-of-the-art words appropriate to the target job. Hit the library. Start building up your technical vocabulary, but don't use any you don't fully understand. All you need are a few choice phrases. This research should not take more than a couple of hours.

You can also glean additional information in the annual reports, catalogues, or other descriptive materials you acquired before the first interview. If you didn't get them, call investor relations, the public relations department, or even your initial interviewer and ask for them.

Do a cram study session like you did before college finals and you'll be ready to wow 'em.

Body Language

If you are introduced personally by the interviewer, the second interview may include him or her. It's up to you to create a "family atmosphere." Watch where you sit. Preferably it should be close to one or both of your "cousins."

The interview will tend to be more familiar and unstructured because of the introduction and the fact that you are back again.

Don't be too physical, but a slightly warmer handshake can work wonders. Powerful thing, touching. But only if you use it sparingly.

Mealtime Interviewing

Although you've been through one fearsome interview, don't look upon the opportunity for a second interview at a meal as a "let down your hair, get to know the boys" opportunity. If you can do so gracefully, avoid the temptation to dine with your prospective employer in favor of a more traditional office meeting. You can do this with a "conflict in schedules" excuse.

Why not sup as you negotiate? Mealtimes are seen as an excellent way to catch the professional, experienced candidate with his or her guard down. Too many things can go wrong. Your careful buildup of corporate cultural knowledge can be overpowered in a room where the decibel level is high. The waiter can make unwelcome intrusions as he asks about "dessert preferences" just as you're launching into a powerfully discreet summation of your candidacy.

Or, in your more relaxed state, you might let "something" slip that you'd never say in a boardroom or office. The opportunity to bring up more "social" topics can be the proverbial thorn in your corporate welcoming bouquet.

On the other hand, an invitation to eat with the executives can be taken as a good sign, because it means you are under serious consideration.

What should you do, then, if you must try to "shine while you dine?"

■ *Food*. Don't order extensively or expensively. Take your cue from the others in your group. If they order steaks, but you never touch red meat, be discreet about your aversion and maybe, just this once, order bite-size brochettes of beef. It doesn't pay to come off sounding like a prim dieter if they're going for the gusto.

Do avoid anything saucy, fish with bones, or finger foods that might wind up on the front of you. Oversauced salads are another risk; ask for dressing on the side, so you can avoid slop-overs.

■ *Alcohol*. Whether the waiter asks or your host prompts, try to graciously decline the opportunity for an alcoholic beverage. Try to stick with club soda with a twist, iced tea, or even plain water.

If pressed, make it mild. A wine spritzer, sherry, or light beer fit this category. Take your cue from others in your party, although you must not appear overly hesitant.

If you do have a drink, limit it to one. If there's an open wine bottle, decline after the first glass by simply placing your hand over the top of the glass. Your waiter will get the message.

■ *Good manners*. Of course, you'll wait until your host begins to eat and stop when he or she does. If your food comes before the host's and he or she urges you to eat, do so without fuss.

When you stop to speak between mouthfuls, cross your knife and fork in the middle of the plate. When you're done with a course, lay the utensils on the plate side by side at the imaginary five o'clock position. Never criticize the food; it impugns your host's choice. Naturally, you must play the perfect guest to a fault, even if the waiter is clumsy, slow, or rude.

Finally, wait for the host to pick up the check. No matter how long it takes, you are not in the position to offer to "split the bill" or "pick up the check." Doing so makes you look as if you don't know proper business etiquette.

Chapter 10

Turning References Into Testimonials

The powerful third-party role of a reference can be either terrible or terrific. A potential employer's check of your references doesn't have to be a test you take blindly and fear you may not pass. It can be a true testimonial. It just depends on you. The key to turning a benign "To whom it may concern" reference into a potent superreference is positioning. The *position* of your reference and the way you are *positioned* by your reference to the reference checker form the elements of a superreference.

Selecting the Right Professional References

Obviously, you should stay away from using your current supervisors as references sources. Successful seekers want to keep their job searches secret.

Review your career history and current business contacts for the names of influential references who can give your search validity without job jeopardy. Consider

- Former supervisors at past employers.
- Your boss's boss and other high-level executives at past employers who know your contributions.
- Coworkers at present or past employers who know your contributions.
- Subordinates who can verify your management ability.
- Colleagues or others who served with you on committees or task forces.
- Members of trade associations or other professional groups who know you.

- Managers of support departments who assisted with your projects. Examples could include managers of finance, management information systems, communications, sales, marketing, market research, purchasing, and inventory control.
- Key employees of consulting firms and other vendors whose services were contracted by your employer and who worked with you directly. Consultants often have contacts and clout, nationwide.
- Key employees of client and supplier companies.

A word of warning. Potential references from the last two categories might want to help, but their own corporate policy could prevent them from doing so. Don't apply pressure. You could destroy future references that would be usable if they were to change jobs.

After you've assembled as comprehensive a list as possible, pick up the phone, smile, and begin calling them. Cross off all the people who greet you with "Bob who?" Cut the call short if the prospective reference sounds mushy mouthed or if he or she greets you in an unfriendly tone. What you want are at least six professional references who are glad to hear from you, and whose word and word skills will help you land that job.

Your reference must mention attributes that get you hired. Let's say one job requires an ability to supervise. You trot out all the references who can attest to your managerial skills. Another job might require analytical skills. Contact the staff accountant from your last job. Call the professor who gave you an "A" in the statistics course you took for your MBA.

Think ahead to all the possible skill areas you'll need in the target job, and keep a reference Rolodex that reflects knowledge of your strengths in specific areas.

Sample Script for Your Call to a Potential Professional Reference

YOU: Joe, good to hear your voice again. It's Sam Stone. Did you get the article I sent you last month on semiconductor research?

JOE: I sure did and I really appreciated it.

YOU: My pleasure. I wasn't sure if you subscribed to that journal and I thought the article might relate to your area. Anyway, I have another reason for calling. I'll only keep you a minute.

I've decided to move on. The reorganization here has led to only limited chances for advancement, so I've decided to look for a director position. This is confidential, of course.

Since we worked together in the past, I'd be honored if you'd provide a professional reference. Your reputation in the industry should help verify my credentials. Will you assist me?

JOE: I'll do my best. [*With such pats on the back, you're bound to get a positive response.*]

YOU: [Briefly mention the objective of your search and the company(ies) you are targeting. Then finish the conversation.] I'll be sending you a couple of items that will help refresh your memory on our work together, and I'll call you back once you've had a chance to scan them. Good talking to you!

Preparing Your Professional References

Your phone calls served as an audition to get you the top four to six colleagues from your professional past or present. Now, you're going to meet with them or talk with them at length (if they're geographically distant), give them their scripts, and coach them into an award-winning performance.

Why bother? Because most of the time your references act anything but professional. They've been caught off guard or may not remember all the highlights you'd like them to recall. But you can be very helpful.

You need to give (or send) four items to each of your references:

1. A sample completed application. (You can either request one from a specific employer or use the generic version from a stationery store that's virtually identical.)
2. The super resume that you created from the tips in Chapter 6.
3. Your individualized reference summary (an example follows).
4. The professional reference questions list.

What's a Reference Summary?

A reference summary is a brief, neatly typed one-page summary, using short headings, that reviews the significant facts that your reference will attest to (see Exhibit 10-1). Concentrate on traits, skills, and accomplishments that apply to the target job.

Be honest, but not modest. Few references will overstate your attributes; most will understate. So give them every word you want them to say, and they may come up with more great thoughts of their own. It's all in the preparation and the careful prompting.

Exhibit 10-1.   Sample reference summary.

Name: John R. Smith

Tel. No: (555) 321-8731

Former Title: National Sales Manager

- Supervised and motivated a field sales force that grew from twelve people to twenty during three-year tenure. Managed and led in-house support staff of six.
- Set and monitored sales objectives by territory and product, resulting in an average annual increase in sales of 30 percent, with an overall three-year cumulative increase of 120 percent (from $6 million in 1985 to $13.2 million in 1988).
- Purchased and installed computerized sales monitoring and reporting system.
- Used customer feedback to help create and market three new products, the AccuSoft, the AccuSort, and the AccuScan, which are consistently among the top sellers produced by the company.
- Established a sales incentive program that increased sales across the board, and more than 50 percent each in the two lowest performing territories.

Traits

- Fast-moving, effective, results-oriented
- Highly skilled at motivating others
- Reliable, loyal, enthusiastic

The Professional Reference Questions List

The final item to give each professional reference is two versions of a list of questions they are likely to be asked in a telephone call. The first version will have "suggested" answers completed by you, to help them remember. Perhaps they never knew you that well when you worked together or the specifics of your job responsibilities. Then give each of your references a copy of a blank list, so they can use the completed one to fill in the blanks in their own words. (They won't bother, but it shows respect on your part.)

Professional Reference Questions

How long have you known _____?
How do you know _____?
When was he/she hired? _____
When did he/she leave? _____

What was his/her salary when he/she left? _____
Did you work with him/her directly? _____
Was he/she absent from work very often? _____
Did his/her personal life ever interfere with his/her work? _____
What were his/her titles? _____
Did he/she cooperate with supervisors? _____
Did he/she cooperate with coworkers? _____
Did he/she take work home very often? _____
What are his/her primary attributes? _____

_____
What are his/her primary liabilities? _____
Is he/she eligible for rehire? _____
Can you confirm the information he/she has given? _____

Overcoming Sensitive Areas and Objections

Review any sensitive areas with the reference. For example, if you were going through a divorce when you worked with your reference and he or she remembers that your personal life interfered with your work, don't leave his or her response to chance. Say something such as:

> "I know I was going through some rough times during that period. I wouldn't have made it without your support. How will you answer questions about my attendance and productivity?"

Need I tell you the answer? Confront a ghost and it vanishes. Fear it, and it haunts your job hunt. People don't tell the truth, even if they want to. They tell their perception of the truth. (People who agree to be references will want to put *your* best foot forward.)

If a reference plainly objects to something you wrote in your preparation materials or remembers the past differently, listen carefully and make changes. It's rare, but you might hear:

> REFERENCE: I don't know about this computerized sales reporting system you say you installed. I know you were involved, but the controller was really responsible. Could we just say you *participated* in choosing and installing a system?"
>
> You: [Graciously and with a smile] Of course. Your way really is more accurate, and still sounds good. That's fine.

When your review is finished, summarize the key points, and tell your references you will notify them of who will be calling, when, and why.

Debriefing Professional References

If you know that you're getting close to a serious offer, call your references and alert them. Make sure they have your materials conveniently close by on their desks.

Communicate with your references throughout your job search. Don't call without a reason, but make brief, time-conscious calls to inquire if they received the expected calls and how the conversations went. Press gently, but firmly, for any key points of discussion. You may want to work them into presentations with other potential employers, if this job doesn't pan out.

One final point. Check to see if they will be available for future calls. You don't want to give the name of a reference who won't be there. If one is traveling on business, ask if he or she will be checking in with the office for messages and returning calls before he or she returns.

Using Professional References for Job Leads

When you contact all your references, you advertise your availability. Some may say, "I know _____, who's in charge of manufacturing [accounting/customer service/management information systems] at _____. Maybe I can put you in touch with him."

Never refuse an offer like that. Even if your references don't offer, ask, because if they can't help you directly, maybe they know someone who can.

Here's one scenario.

Judy was stalled in her job as a writer of programming manuals for a small East Coast software manufacturer. She had been with the company for three years and had been promoted to supervisor of her department of four writers and a technical editor.

Although her undergraduate degree was in computer science, she'd studied at night to complete an MBA with an emphasis in marketing. Judy believed that her education, combined with her knowledge of user needs, prepared her for a marketing manager position. But her company had only one such position, and it didn't look as if it would be vacant soon.

So Judy decided to review her contacts to find a few superstars who could become superreferences. She wanted them to supercharge her into a bigger company where she could maximize her marketing training. She decided on:

- *Judd,* a former coworker, who left to start a small software company. Although Judd's company only had a few products, one of them had recently been successful and was getting loads of industry attention. His letterhead read "Justin Davis, President, Specialized Software Corporation" with a prestigious Los Angeles address.
- Then there was *Elizabeth,* a marketing manager of computer peripherals whom Judy had met at a conference; and
- *Dr. William Dutton,* an adjunct faculty member at the graduate school of business where Judy had studied, a former government official, and the director of competitive intelligence for a defense manufacturing company. Judy took Dr. Dutton's course in competitive intelligence and business marketing. They became friends and she even helped him prepare a manuscript.

Judy's three principal references had a wealth of contacts in the software marketing business who could help her target marketing directors of manufacturers. The letters they wrote to introduce her and direct attention to her resume won her interview after interview. She had four reference-influenced offers and today she's rapidly climbing the marketing ladder at one of the world's biggest software manufacturers. "Even if you don't know any highly placed officials or company presidents, somewhere among your contacts there is someone who will write a credible cover letter to get your resume read, your interview set, and your job offered."

Consider your professional references as your lifetime lifeline. Advise them when you get your desired position. Express your appreciation in a phone call (a letter is even better) and promptly send a tasteful but not too expensive thank-you gift. Be sure to let them know you'll willingly serve in the same capacity when they mount job searches. Keep in occasional touch and tell them of your progress. If it worked once, it can work again, as they become sources for future job advancement.

Essentials for Professional Reference Letters

You want to ensure that the letter writer is able to do you some good. He or she should be a preference reference like Judy. A preference reference fits any one of the following key characteristics:

- The reference knows the recipient of the letter.
- The reference knows someone else the recipient knows.

- The reference is someone who, by reputation, is known to the recipient of the letter.
- The reference is someone whose letterhead and title will attract the recipient's attention or give credibility to the statements and to you.
- The writer of the letter should hold an equal or superior position to the recipient. An exception might be when the letter is written by a former employee who has a good relationship with his or her former boss. Another exception might be when the reference is on good terms with a higher-level executive from any other company whom he or she met at a conference.

Request that your reference prepare a letter that (a) positions its writer as an authority, (b) is directed to the person holding the proper position within the proper company, and (c) is written to position you as an indispensable product offering an exceptional service. It may also subtly remind the recipient of favors past or promised. See the example shown in Exhibit 10-2.

Selecting the Right Personal References

Personal references used to be snubbed by placement professionals. For years, the names dutifully listed under Personal References were people no self-respecting employer would call because they were thought to have a vested interest in talking up the attributes of the candidate.

No more. With all the legal and business restraints now limiting what a company can say about a former employee, personal references are an important addition to your list of professionals. In fact, they're becoming preference references.

The interviewer will call the references and receive an enthusiastic in-depth response that can't be equalled by professional references.

Each of your personal references should:

1. Formally consent to give a reference about you
2. Have a different surname from you (even if related)
3. Work in an office where he or she can receive calls during regular business hours without distraction and discuss you knowledgeably, intelligently, and enthusiastically

Begin by listing fifty possibles on a sheet of paper. From them you'll cut the list down to the top five.

Exhibit 10-2. Sample professional letter.

AMERICAN FOODS COMPANY
2204 Mercantile Building
Chicago, Illinois 60626
(555) 974-0700

Angela P. Edwards, Director
Market Research

April 3, 1995

Margaret O. Blaine, Product Manager
Convenience Foods Division
American Foods Company
1667 Commonwealth Avenue
Boston, MA 02210

Re: Amanda F. Harston Reference

Dear Marge:

I hope all is going well with your new product launch. Last November, when my department gave you that revised market research you needed, you asked me to let you know if you could return the favor. Well, now you can.

My associate and friend, Amanda Harston, is applying for the assistant product manager position that opened at the breakfast division of American. In addition to great credentials, Amanda has the energy, insight, and dedication needed to be an outstanding assistant product manager.

As the enclosed resume shows, Amanda recently enhanced her ten years' experience in product marketing at XYZ, Inc., with an MBA from Bentley College. She graduated with high honors in spite of a sixty-hour-per-week job that required 70 percent travel.

Although she has moved up steadily at XYZ, now that she has solid experience and graduate credentials, she'd like a larger environment.

I know John Lawson, who is hiring for this position, will interview Amanda if the request comes from you. It won't be a waste of time. In fact, John will probably feel he owes you a favor once he meets Amanda. Please pass her resume along to him; she'll call John for an interview by the end of the week. Thanks in advance for your assistance.

Best regards,

Angela P. Edwards
Enclosure

Where do you get a list of fifty? Personal friends. Casual acquaintances. Then add business advisors such as your attorney, accountant, or banker. Maybe you've recently purchased a house—your real estate agent is a natural. How about community leaders, members of your service club or health club? Are there teachers at your children's school with whom you have special rapport? Jot them down.

What characteristics do you need in each of your top five?

- A successful business or professional life
- A self-confident, outgoing personality
- Good oral skills

Although personal references can be located anywhere, it helps your cause if they're in the community where you're conducting your job search. You can leverage their favorable reputations and often the reference checker will more readily want to speak with prominent people in the area.

If you've kept your personal life close to the vest, don't worry. Getting references from people who don't know you well may be easier than getting them from people who do. Casual acquaintances have fewer or no negative impressions to recall.

In picking the top five from fifty, choose those most likely to be receptive immediately to your request, accessible, and properly positioned to help turn calls into job offers. Like professional references, your personal references will be complimented that you want them to speak up for you.

Try a script similar to the following between Betty, a job seeker, and Howard, an attorney who lives in her neighborhood.

BETTY: "Howard, this is Betty Brown."

HOWARD: "Hi, Betty. I've been meaning to call and ask you what you're using on your roses this year. They look great."

BETTY: "Why, thank you! I'll have to refer that question to the family gardener. Frank takes care of the yard."

HOWARD: "I'd really like to know. I haven't had any luck with mine. What can I do for you?"

BETTY: "Well, I just passed the CPA exam, and I want to make a career move now. Foster Plastics is a great company, and it was convenient to work in town while the kids were young. But now I'm ready for a larger organization. I thought I'd target the insurance industry."

HOWARD: "Sounds good. Congratulations on your certification.

That was a lot of work. I wish I knew someone to recommend. I'm afraid I can't be much help."

BETTY: "Howard, you can be a big help. I'd like to use your name as a personal reference. We worked closely together on last year's school budget campaign, and I was impressed by your energy, your effectiveness, and your ability to communicate. I hoped your observations of me were equally good and that you wouldn't mind saying so to a prospective employer."

HOWARD: "I'm honored to be asked! I couldn't have done all I did without your assistance in supplying the numbers to support our arguments. Talk about analytical skill! The Board of Ed is still talking about your accuracy!"

Overcoming Objections

Since we don't live in an ideal world and not everyone is as obliging as Howard in the sample script, there will be individuals who may not want to be your personal reference, because:

"I've never given a reference before."
"I'm not sure how to go about it."
"I'm afraid I'll say something wrong."

To overcome these objections, reassure them that you're going to provide them with a sample application, your resume, and a list of questions typically asked. Tell them you'll go over the key points that you want them to cover, and if they'll just review the materials and answer naturally, "It will all go fine."

To all reluctant references, express the importance of their help and how much you appreciate it. If they still seem hesitant, thank them and allow them to beg off gracefully. You want references with genuine enthusiasm. The last thing you need is for your future employer to sense that someone is only doing this as a favor to you.

Preparing Your Personal References

The steps to follow are very similar to those for preparing your professional references. Your *personal references* need

- Your resume
- The reference summary
- The personal reference questions list

The Reference Summary

For personal references, this summary is simply a one-page list describing your attributes and activities that (1) the reference can authenticate and (2) are relevant to your target job. Exhibit 10-3 is the summary that Betty Brown gave to Howard, her personal reference.

Based on the format in Exhibit 10-3, you should prepare a similar summary to give to each of your references. Be sure your references understand and agree with its contents. Don't be shy about your attributes. Your references would rather have correct information on what to say than risk messing up.

As you review the summary as you have tailored it for each reference, make sure that he or she understands:

- Your job search objectives
- Specifically what you want him or her to say in a reference call
- The proper tone of voice for maximum impact

If you're targeting more than one job, the reference should be given two or more summaries. Each should be clearly marked so your reference knows what to say to whom.

Exhibit 10-3. Sample reference summary.

Name: Betty R. Brown

Telephone No. (616) 555-3359

Position Desired: Accountant Insurance Company

CHARACTER TRAITS

- Determination
- Accuracy
- Thoroughness
- Commitment
- Follow-through
- Energy
- Enthusiasm
- Competence
- Positive Attitude

JOB-RELATED ABILITIES AND SKILLS

- Compiled financial data and developed complete, accurate forecasts
- Presented concise, understandable financial reports for budget projections
- Demonstrated knowledge of accounting principles and procedures

It's important that each reference have a slightly different summary, even though it means more work for you. Otherwise all might come out sounding exactly the same about you. Canned responses won't get you the job; you need each reference to answer with the appearance of spontaneity, candor, and enthusiasm.

The Personal Reference Questions List

Again, like professional references, your personal references should be given a list of probable questions (see Exhibit 10-4). Each should get two copies—one with suggested answers written by you, the other blank to let your references mesh the "correct" answers with their own personal versions.

The answers should help refresh your personal references' recollections about the dates and details of your relationship and to make sure that what you say is verified by what they say.

Defusing Potential Trouble Spots

What is said to the reference checker is too important to be left unsaid by you. Even well-meaning references can reply inappropriately when they're unprepared.

Look carefully at the list in Exhibit 10-4. It contains loaded questions: Is (he/she) easy to get along with? What are (his/her) primary liabilities? Your coaching should prepare your references to avoid these potential minefields. The completed reference summary prepared your references to discuss your attributes. You can help them

Exhibit 10-4. Personal reference questions.

How long have you known _____ ?
How do you know _____ ?
What is your opinion of _____ ?
Does (he/she) get along well with others? _____
Is (he/she) usually on time? _____
Is (he/she) absent from work very often? _____
Does (he/she) bring work home very often? _____
Does (he/she) like (his/her) job? _____
What are (his/her) primary attributes?

What are (his/her) primary liabilities? _____

handle the question about liabilities equally well. Here are some answers that can transform liabilities into assets:

> "Well, the one liability that comes to mind is that she considers herself last. She's never too busy to help someone or volunteer for another position. She's one of those people who proves the truth of the phrase 'If you want it done, give it to a busy person.' It's funny, though. She never seems to get ruffled about it all. She's organized, efficient, and goal-oriented. It seems the more she does, the happier she is."

> "His liabilities? Oh, I guess you could say he's a workaholic. He's canceled our Saturday morning tennis game on several occasions because he wanted to work on his projects while the office was quiet. Completing his work has consistently been his top priority. He's very dedicated."

Always end a discussion of a liability or weakness by turning it into an attribute or strength.

"Is (he/she) easy to get along with?" can be a loaded question. Someone can be too easy if he or she is unable to say no. In this case, the answer would be:

> "(He/She) is firm, but fair. I've never seen (him/her) arbitrary; instead (he/she) sets reasonable rules and expects them to be upheld. I've always found (him/her) very likable and concerned about the welfare of others, but (he/she) is no pushover."

These are your friends. Arrange for enough time to explain your objectives and show your references how they can help you achieve them. Meet personally over a quiet lunch or dinner (your treat, of course), and let them know how important this is to you. Give them your carefully prepared information, and review it in detail.

Resist the temptation to give in when a personal reference says: "Hey, I don't need your resume or any of this paperwork. I'll just tell them a bunch of lies. Don't worry. You'll sound great!"

Explain that it is important to you to sound great with the facts, and only those closest to you know just how to express them.

Debriefing Your Personal References

Ask your references to accept telephone calls or to return them immediately. Of course, you'll offer to pay any toll charges. Have them notify you of the details the moment they hang up. You need the feedback now so you can prepare for your next interview.

Using Personal References for Other Job Leads

Once a reference gets involved with you, she feels as though she has a vested interest in your success.

Your background information can get this reference to see you in a new light. Previously a friend or acquaintance, now you are a professional with credentials. The reference may have contacts that can work in your favor to secure additional job leads.

You don't want to push your personal references too far since they're doing you the initial great service of speaking on your behalf. However, if you can work your way around to the subject or if they say, "You know, after looking at your resume, I've got a friend you should talk to," then by all means follow up.

Chapter 11

An Employment Agreement

Employment agreements are designed to objectively clarify the employment relationship. For the second decade employee, promotion opportunities and job security represent bottom line considerations. For the employer, protection against liability for breaching preemployment promises, discrimination, and wrongful termination is becoming essential. The terms vary greatly, but the objectives for both parties do not.

The Employment Insurance Policy for Your Next Decade

You may wonder, "Won't the employer feel it's presumptuous of me and that I have a lack of good faith if I bring up the subject of a contract?" Few top executives join a company without such a document, and the employment contract is increasingly filtering down to the mid-level ranks. The trick is to know how to negotiate it. Is it worth sailing on relatively uncharted waters to test acceptance by your potential employer? The answer is yes, if:

- The industry is volatile or has a history of rapid run-ups and declines
- The company is ready to go on the block for acquisition or merger
- The company has a reputation for picking the brains of its employees and then casting them aside
- It's a closely held family-owned company

I've seen numbers tossed around, but by today's standards, if your gross annual salary ranges upward from $60,000, you really should consider an agreement.

144

Employment Agreement Provisions

If you attempt to write the contract in advanced legalese, you can be sure the corporate attorneys will look at it so long and hard that your candidacy will be moot. Here is an effective initial paragraph that is clear and to the point:

Sample Paragraph

In consideration of [*name of employer*] (Employer) hiring [*first and last name of employee*] (Employee), it is agreed as follows:

A gross amount of $_____ per _____ shall be paid by Employer to Employee, less any customary and usual deductions for the performances in the initial position of _____. Said gross amount shall be increased by at least _____ before the anniversary date of Employee. Changes in status or promotions shall be at the sole discretion of Employer.

Place this paragraph on the first page of the agreement. It is particularly important that it look sharp and stand out, since it discusses the bottom line—money. Leave the percentage of increase blank, since by inserting the number, the supervisor will feel that he has negotiated the agreement. This single device has been one of the most effective means to get the employer to sign. It really gives up nothing, since invariably a supervisor will insert an amount approximately two percentage points higher than the cost of living. Don't ask me why, but that's the phenomenon of contemplating salary and letting the employer negotiate against himself.

Don't overwrite the contract; here is what comes next:

Sample Paragraph

If Employer terminates the employment of Employee after ninety (90) days for any reason other than a specific violation of a written policy acknowledged by Employee, _____ times the current weekly gross amount shall be immediately paid to Employee. Said amount includes pay in lieu of notice and severance pay but excludes any personal leave, holiday, vacation, or other pro rata pay in accordance with the policy of Employer.

You need to determine and insert the amount of severance pay. If you can get the information by a quick, anonymous call to human relations, do so. Then double the amount. Otherwise, four weeks is generally the maximum a new hire can receive.

Aside from equal employment opportunity laws, your employment is still basically terminable at will. You can't and shouldn't fight city hall on this one or the agreement will never be signed, and you may become candidate non grata.

The next paragraph is a great way to proclaim your professional ethics. It simply states existing case law at federal and state levels and shows your good faith. It is also a way to avoid liability for unfair competition if you leave. Employers are notoriously paranoid about the extent of their trade secrets and by acknowledging this you demonstrate your concern.

Sample Paragraph

Employee acknowledges that the internal procedures, records, files, lists, forms, and other proprietary information developed or obtained by Employer in the course of its business operations are confidential trade secrets, and shall remain the exclusive property of Employer. Accordingly, Employee shall not retain, duplicate, disclose, or use any of said information, except in furtherance of the employment.

This single paragraph accounts for a large number of agreements being signed and is often adopted later by employers for all employees. So you're already leading the way!

Known as a best efforts paragraph, the following paragraph is standard fare in employment agreements.

Sample Paragraph

Employee agrees to act in an attractive, ethical, and responsible manner, and to exclusively represent Employer at all times with the utmost concern for its goals, interests, and image with employees, suppliers, customers, and members of the general public.

The next paragraph is a very important paragraph for you, since it is very likely that the employer can better afford to litigate a dispute through the courts than you can. You don't want to spend years, wipe out your life savings, or abandon a just claim, just because you can't afford it. Binding arbitration is a relatively painless, inexpensive, and realistic way to resolve disputes. The American Arbitration Association's rules are traditionally accepted and considered fair.

Sample Paragraph

If it becomes necessary for Employee or Employer to enforce or interpret the terms of this Agreement, the matter shall be settled by binding arbitration under the auspices and in accordance with the rule of the American Arbitration Association. Judgment on the award rendered may be entered in any court of competent jurisdiction.

It serves your best interests to keep the world at large from knowing of this agreement, thus the final paragraph of the agreement. Adding date and signature lines is a good way to ensure that it will be signed.

Sample Paragraph

Neither Employee nor Employer shall disclose either the existence of this Agreement or any of its terms for the duration of the employment. If Employee shall directly or indirectly cause such disclosure, Employer may immediately terminate the employment, as though a written policy formally acknowledged by the Employee had been violated.

Sample Date and Signature Lines

Dated: _____ 19 ____

Employer: _____
Name of Employer

By: _____
Signature

Title: _____

Employee: _____
Signature

Although a formal agreement has more psychological impact, a letter agreement is just as valid. Of course, nothing is valid if it's not signed, so if you believe a letter agreement will fly more readily, the following should appear after your signature:

The Above Terms Are Hereby Accepted.

Dated: _____, 19 ____

_____ (name of employer) _____
(Employer)

By: _____ (first name, last name) _____

Title: _____

If you have arranged a consulting assignment, you can use the same format, changing *Employee* to *Consultant,* and eliminating any reference to employment or employee benefits.

Another Option: The Severance Agreement

Recently, there has also been considerable interest in severance agreements as substitutes for employment contracts. They are usually short letters in which an employer agrees to provide an irrevocable severance compensation package. Again, these work well for executives in the $60,000+ annual salary range.

Usually such agreements provide six months salary, relocation expenses, insurance benefits for twelve months, and professional outplacement. In this case, the agreement you sign should cover any and all situations by which your employment is terminated.

How to Get Your Employment Agreement Signed

When it comes to getting your employment contract signed, you'll be in good shape by using the Perfect Four Ps—Person, Proper Timing, Presentation, and Packaging.

1. *Person.* You don't want to preach the gospel to an employment interviewer. It's not his or her domain. Make certain you're talking with a decision maker; otherwise you're just wasting your time.

2. *Proper timing.* Once you've successfully negotiated the terms of your compensation, more or less you're sitting in the driver's seat, however temporarily. So you must get the document signed before reporting for work. Approximately 80 percent of all employment agreements are executed prior to an employee's start date. Make your move regarding the contract as soon as the job is offered. It can be one of your major stipulations in joining the company.

3. *Presentation.* There's a predictable flow to bringing up the subject of an employment contract. This predictability makes the situation so controllable. Here is one such scenario:

SUPERVISOR: Well, I guess you've gathered that we're interested in having you come to work for us. How does it sound to you?
YOU: It sounds like an ideal position for me to use my experience productively.

SUPERVISOR: We've decided to offer you the position of manager of consumer affairs, starting at $60,000. This will allow for additional increases within the rate range. Your performance will be reviewed in ninety days, and you will be eligible for a merit increase after six months. I assume you've discussed our annual review policy and company benefits with human relations.

YOU: Yes, I have. The salary sounds fine, and the opportunity is exactly what I've been seeking. Don't you think we should prepare a short agreement outlining the terms? (An inverted tie-down; see Chapter 8.)

SUPERVISOR: We've never used them, and our corporate attorney is very conservative. We think we've got a good match here, and I'd really like to wrap this thing up.

YOU: I agree. I'm anxious to assist you. Why don't I either bring the agreement to you at nine tomorrow morning, or leave it with the receptionist? Then we can discuss it. Of course, it will be in a sealed envelope marked Confidential. I'm preparing it myself. It's really just a memorandum of understanding.

SUPERVISOR: Well, OK. I'll speak to the vice president of administration and see if I can get approval in advance. When can you start? (A major concession!)

YOU: I should give my present employer two weeks' notice. My boss would appreciate that, since I have major responsibilities. If you like, I'll explain that you need me right away and leave it up to him. Once he recovers from shock, I'm sure he'll understand.

SUPERVISOR: It would really help me out. We've been inundated with inquiries from customers.

YOU: No problem. I've handled these successfully in the past. Why don't I take some files with me? I'm anxious to get started.

SUPERVISOR: Fine. Jeanne will take you to the consumer affairs department, and we'll find some homework for you.

YOU: Great. (Magic Four Goodbye time—see Chapter 8.) I'll leave the papers with the receptionist in the morning.

SUPERVISOR: OK. I'll call you in the afternoon when they're approved, and you can give notice.

Notice the tone of the conversation. It's optimistic, enthusiastic, and action oriented. No talk about running to a lawyer. It's just a mere formality.

The meeting really can go this smoothly, and you can find yourself subtly in control.

4. *Packaging.* If you follow the simple, succinct format in the previous pages for packaging your employment agreement, your chances of getting it signed will be enormously enhanced.

Chapter 12

How to Become Relentlessly Recruited

By the time you reach the second decade of your career, you should have received some recognition (not notoriety, but quiet respect). An array of talent seekers who use a variety of names should come calling on you. You'll recognize them as executive recruiters or their alter egos (professional/management/technical recruiters, executive/professional/management/technical search firms, executive/professional management/technical consultants, headhunters, etc.).

How Employment Recruiting Has Changed Over the Last Decade

With all these terms, it's confusing to know what to look for. The best way to begin is to understand the extremely competitive marketplace inhabited by these firms.

In the private, for-profit sector where the bulk of the best jobs lie, there are three primary types of employment services:

- Permanent employment agencies where you pay the fee.
- Permanent employment agencies where the employer pays the fee.
- Contingency and retained search firms.

Differences Between Employment Agencies and Search Firms

Employment agencies in the private sector must be registered as either Employee Paid Fee (EPF) or Applicant Paid Fee (APF, now becoming increasingly rare).

Before you sign on the dotted line for representation, make sure you know who pays the fee. The great strength of employment agencies is their street smarts, unpretentiousness, and flexibility. Because their consultants-on-commission achieve placements more frequently than recruiters, they're used to working with a larger inventory of candidates and job orders.

You should be aware that only employment agencies and certain contingency search firms will market you to a large number of employers. Even then, they may or may not have an existing relationship with these firms. Executive search firms simply present your credentials. (That's not bad. With the blessing of the right headhunter, you've got the advantage of walking in from the "right door.")

In *Executive Search*, Richard Connaroe explains the difference between the traditional employment agency and the headhunters. "The basic mission of an employment agency is to find jobs for candidates. This approach is not appropriate, however, for senior-level management positions where the mission is to find candidates for jobs with very exciting and stringent requirements."

Yet, with the increasing professionalism of the placement industry, the expansion of employer-paid firms, and more sophisticated applicants, most executive recruiters and employment agencies actually perform the same functions in the same way.

For this reason, many excellent jobs for second-decade defenders fall in the purview of employent agencies. That's especially true if your earnings range is currently under $60,000.

Criteria for Selecting an Employment Agency

- Check on when the firm began. If they've been in business since you were in school, it's likely you can count on them for the long haul.
- Are they affiliated with professional associations? In the employment field, the leading trade organization is the National Association of Personnel Consultants, active in all fifty states.
- Being a franchisee of an employment agency chain can also be a powerful plus. Names such as Dunhill and Snelling & Snelling are recognized and respected nationwide. With their national databases, that's an important factor if you're planning to move.
- Ask if your prospective consultant has CPC status. CPC stands for certified placement counselor—a designation recognized for professionalism based on rigorous training and study. Generally an individual who has achieved CPC standing has at least five years' experience.

Can You Select an Executive Search Firm?

There are two definite schools of thought regarding search firms. Some will argue that executive search firms prefer to locate you out of a talent pool, based on their own research. It's a strange jungle where you're the quarry (read *candidate*) stalking the hunter (head-hunter, and ultimately, the employer).

Others say it's OK to make the contact yourself. In *How to Survive Getting Fired—and Win,* placement executive Paul Norrell comments, "It's a common misunderstanding that executive search companies aren't interested. . . . We're [just] highly selective. We want to send the best possible candidate to our clients."

How Executive Recruiters Work

Search businesses are often owned by management, technical, and sales executives from various industries, who specialize in certain occupations, industries, or geographic areas.

Recruiters are successful because they know where the action is in the job market. They know employers from the inside, including their intramural politics and the state of corporate morale. They know who has exciting products on the drawing boards and who's about to lose employees. They know who has high turnover and who pays well.

Most of their leads come from people they know and trust. With specialization comes in-depth research. This way, the recruiters provide themselves with prospects and leads for future openings. For example, if an executive search firm is on a retainer to supply Microsoft with candidates, you can bet they'll be in Silicon Valley (Calif.) and Washington state on a regular basis. They'll find out who the best people are and who may be agreeable to a good offer.

Executive recruiters are paid by the employer (client). Only about 5 percent are actually paid to identify and recruit qualified candidates for a specific position. In 95 percent of the cases, the recruiter has either no specific job order at all or has one for a contingency fee, nonexclusive job order. The placement fee is usually one percent per thousand dollars of the employee's projected first year salary. The competitive nature of the business makes it unlikely you'll get career counseling here.

Headhunters usually compete with several other similar firms (plus the employer) to fill the position as quickly as possible. Their office managers and recruiters are compensated based on the placement fees received, or "cash in." Some (particularly the refugees from human resource departments) use big words. Most know the ropes and the rules. You have to impress them before you'll become a "send-out" to their clients. They're only as good as their last placements.

Executive recruiters tend to be clustered in major cities and can be found in the Yellow Pages. Look under Executive Recruiting Consultants, Management Consultants, Personnel Consultants or variations on these themes.

If you contact them, be prepared to send your best efforts—cover letter, resume, and any publicity clippings about your achievements from corporate newsletters, trade journals, or even the consumer press.

Select no more than two or three who cover your field. Because they are in the employment intelligence business, they soon learn if you're peddling yourself all over town (or even nationwide). Then they'll avoid you like the plague.

If the consultant is interested in you, be totally honest. You'll be asked for a detailed analysis of your job duties, accomplishments, and education. Explain any problem areas. (You don't want to leave them, and ultimately yourself, holding the bag.)

How to Increase Your Hireability

Because headhunters are most interested in executives who are currently employed, they gather information by asking others working in the industry.

Your first contact with a headhunter may be in the form of a phone call or letter at the office. He or she will focus on a description of a specific position and ask if you can recommend anyone qualified for it.

If you don't want to discuss the matter at work, ask the consultant to call you at home, after business hours. They're used to doing this.

If you are interested in the job, say so, but don't appear over eager. Playing it cool will make you more desirable to consultants used to wooing people who already have jobs, and who, in many cases, have reservations about making a change.

Don't disregard the opportunity to communicate with the headhunter, even if you plan to stay where you are. By supplying names of other potential candidates, you make yourself known to the recruitment firm. Then when you're ready to move on, you'll have important name recognition, at the very least.

When you make such a recommendation, be sure to jot down the name of the agency and the recruiter. Date it, and write down the name of the candidate you suggested. This information can form the basis of your initial contact with the firm later. (Naturally, such sensitive information belongs at home—never at work.)

Increase Your Visibility: Get Your Name in Print

Headhunters devour newspapers, business journals, magazines, company newsletters, and every other avenue for possible candidates and job leads. The key is to get your name in print for something positive.

Company newsletters are a natural. The editor is always looking for something to write about. It's so difficult to find staff contributors that I used to ghost write the entire newsletter, then find people who'd consent to having their names used.

Headhunters receive smuggled copies of these internal house organs all the time. They contain names, faces, titles, personal backgrounds, company news, industry trends, and many other items that provide the grist of the headhunters' basic commodity—talented flesh.

Volunteer to write for your internal newspaper and you'll be twice blessed. The editor will love you for it and word will filter back to your boss. It also becomes a tradeable commodity in the executive recruiting field—tradeable in terms of getting yourself known.

Write Company Memos

Company memos are undoubtedly the most overlooked public relations device ever written. Even when they're not surreptitiously dropped into the hands of waiting recruiters, they are the high visibility form of internal communication. Anyone can write them, control their content, and aim them squarely at the target. How much more potent could a public relations device be?

A public relations memo has only five components, but all must be there. They include:

1. *Predetermined format.* Use it. By setting up the title (Memorandum, Interoffice Memorandum, Memo, etc.) and the To, From, Date, and Subject or Re lines the customary way in your organization, you'll maximize the acceptability of the content. If there is none, just use the traditional form by aligning each item on the upper left, as follows:

```
To:
From:
Date:
Subject:
```

2. *Topic sentence*. The first sentence, the topic sentence, should be short, concise, and to the point. Examples are:

> I am pleased to inform you that the operations group has stream-lined the procedure for ordering office supplies.

> During the next few weeks, we will be concentrating on ways to increase the responsiveness to customer inquiries.

> As we discussed by phone today, a patent has just been issued for the data retrieval system I developed.

3. *Short body*. It should be under one page. A public relations memo reflects you, so make it crisp and to the point. Write it out first. Then work with it—fight your way through it again. Cross out excess words and phrases (*that, and, or, and/or, as you know*, etc.). Include short, direct words (*use* instead of *utilize, buy* instead of *purchase*, etc.). It should not contain:

> More than three paragraphs
> More than three simple sentences per paragraph
> Words with more than three syllables

Keep it short, sweet, and simple. People are preoccupied, and the more paper that crosses their desks, the more irritated they become. Write good news—management appreciates it. So do recruiters. Write from the reader's point of view. Egos and opinions need to be stroked and cultivated.

4. *Accents, exclamations, and triggers*. Successful people don't talk in a monotone. They punctuate what they say and people listen. Your one-page memo should underline a few key words or phrases. It should contain one exclamation point at the end of no more than two sentences. It should contain words that move and shake such as *expedite, improve*, or *perform*.

5. *Concluding sentence*. The concluding sentence should be one short sentence. Enough said. Here are examples:

> Thanks again for your assistance!

We'll let you know the results as they are received.

I hope this success will reflect favorably on our company!

Contribute to Trade Publications

Every field has its own core of trade publications. We discussed that earlier in Chapter 5. If you don't know the key players in your area, shame on you. In the meantime, go to the library and consult *Bacon's Publicity Checker*. It's a two-volume set. Ask for the one listing magazines.

To suggest a topic to a trade paper or magazine, check the name of the current editor. Then do what professional freelance writers do: Send a short pitch letter such as the one in Exhibit 12-1. Your letter should not be more than one page long and should not contain:

More than three paragraphs
More than three simple sentences per paragraph
Complex, indecisive words that don't make a point

What should you write about? Do what every columnist and author does; write about what interests you. You can write a "how to" article, profile a new discovery, or survey your colleagues—anything practical or relevant right now.

Of course, if the piece is already written, you can include it. Don't worry about it being used without attribution; just worry about it being used. You can include a two-line brief biography about yourself, and it will probably be printed without any editing. Don't worry about getting paid. Your remuneration comes from others seeing your name in print.

Once you've written for these insatiably hungry specialty publishers, you might want to submit editorial variations to mass-market media. If so, go directly to your local bookstore and buy a copy of the latest *Writer's Market* (Cincinnati: Writer's Digest Books). It's an annually updated, reasonably priced book that's like a Yellow Pages of publishers. In addition, it summarizes what each publisher wants and includes hints on how to prepare ideas and manuscripts. There are over 4,000 names, addresses, phone numbers, and preferences of publishers looking for submissions. Just make sure you have the latest copy. The changes in the printing field are faster than in almost any other job market.

Sometimes local newspapers hire freelance writers for feature stories. With your unique perspective, you never know what will see the printer's light of day. That's especially true for smaller home town

Exhibit 12-1.   Trade article pitch letter.

ROGER L. NORTON
3271 Airway Avenue
Brighton, MA 25706

July 16, 1995

American Association of Contract Administrators
4038 Gramatan Road
Long Beach, DE 98368

Attn: David N. Stafford, Executive Director

Re: Article for *Contract Administration Review*

I have a feature article in mind for *Contract Administration Review* entitled "Latest Techniques for Negotiating Office Leases."

As a senior contract administrator with Henley Investment Corporation, for eight years I have specialized in lease negotiations. Now there are many new developments in fixed and variable leases for offices. Accordingly this article should be both interesting and informative to AACA members.

I will call you within the next week to discuss it further and look forward to contributing to *Contract Administration Review*.

Thank you for your anticipated consideration.

Very truly yours,

ROGER L. NORTON

RLN: aja

---

papers. All you care about is that it's something local headhunters will read. Also submit news of a promotion, job change, or assumption of new responsibilities. Larger metropolitan dailies usually won't use this, but smaller papers will. A good, current photo wouldn't hurt, either.

Join, Attend, and Contact

Anything that gets your name around will help you get caught by a headhunter. Attending trade association meetings is fine but can waste your time if you're really looking to make a move soon. As part of an ongoing career strategy, though, do it.

One of the benefits of joining may be a directory put out by the association listing their members' names and affiliations. All the better if it is circulated beyond the existing membership. Business-to-business advertisers may buy such a directory. So will headhunters. It's part of their hunting gear.

Check *The Directory of Executive Search Firms* by William Lewis and Carol Milano (New York: Prentice-Hall, 1986) and *The Directory of Executive Recruiters* by James Kennedy (Fitzwilliam, N.H.: Consultants News, 1994). Some successful headhunters work out of their homes. Regardless of their location or size, many recruiters are members of computerized personnel networks. These have massive databases of clients and candidates. Being in them is like having your career on automatic pilot, straight up.

You owe it to yourself to know a cadre of headhunters. They have a native's understanding of the job market and an objective knowledge of employers. From candidates, cold calls, job orders, industry directories, annual reports, trade shows, and hundreds of other sources, they develop a sixth-sense understanding of the games, the plays, the players, and the scores. Whether it's to confirm you're in the right place, to find out what's happening there, or to suggest alternatives, they're the best.

Once you get your foot in their door, your head couldn't be in better hands.

Chapter 13

Building a Network to Get Work

Networking was the darling of the late 1970s through the mid 1980s. Then because the term had been misused, misapplied, and simply ground up in the stampede into formal and informal career networks, pretty soon networking started to get in the way of working. Eventually people simply went back to "getworking" again.

Networking has always been around and always will be. When your parents were job hunting, if they fell into a good position, one good reason might have been that they were well connected. Remember them telling you, "It's not what you know, it's who you know"? All those old platitudes still mean the same thing—networking.

In *Job Search: The Total System*, authors Kenneth and Sheryl Dawson comment,

> Just because networking is misused, abused and trivialized by amateurs doesn't mean that you must choose an alternative. Quite simply, there are none. U.S. Department of Labor statistics prove that 80 percent of people who find jobs in this country do so by networking. . . . Effective networking gets jobs. The more you do it and the better you do it, the sooner you'll be selecting the best positions from among several offers.

In its recent "Jobs in America" section, *Fortune* concurred, stating,

> In this new age of impermanence and uncertainty, staying in touch—with colleagues, friends, neighbors, customers, suppliers—is one of the keys to keeping yourself employable . . . most people find new jobs not by sending out resumes or responding to want ads, but by using connections. In other words, by networking.

As with all art forms, and good networking is certainly an art, you have to learn the basics before you can master it and tap its rewards. Fortunately, it's not difficult.

In their book, *Electronic Resume Revolution,* Joyce Lain Kennedy and Thomas J. Morrow suggest that the most productive networking is more than calling up friends to see if they've heard about any available jobs. They say, "Real networking is carefully tended give and take. It's the favor bank into which you make regular deposits as take withdrawals. The best networkers practice their preventive networking art over years of concern and caring for their contacts."

What Do You Want From Contacts?

Even before you make up your list of contacts, think about what you want from them. This will go a long way to clarifying the purpose of your calls. Ideally, your contacts should be people who can do one or more of the following:

- Offer you a job.
- Refer you to someone who can arrange an interview.
- Notify you about opportunities. Their motivation to assist is best used by asking them to be your eyes and ears. Helping you enhances their own self-esteem. They often delight in letting you know inside information or leads discovered through personal observation.
- Present your background. Particularly in high-level executive positions, personal recommendations count more than anything else.
- Give you the names of people who can help you in one or more of the above areas.

Begin With Informal Contacts

Cast the *net* part of your networking effort far and wide—at least initially. Begin by making a comprehensive list of possible contacts. You probably won't use them all but it's good to have them on a single available list with name and phone number. Who should be on it?

- *Family.* Immediate and extended, including parents, siblings, in-laws, aunts, uncles, and cousins.

• *Friends from the past*. Neighbors, customers, military friends, college chums. Just don't go back so far that their memory of you is distant. About ten years is a good benchmark. Even if they can't help you now, bringing them up to date and telling them where you are and what you're doing plants seeds that may sprout in the future. Coworkers from the past are an especially fertile field. The potential for interview contacts aside, former colleagues and supervisors can be valuable references.

• *Current friends and neighbors*. They may work for a company that encourages networking referrals. Some companies are so convinced that their best employees have been referred by a current employee, they offer up to four-figure bonuses for introducing candidates who are hired and retained on the job for a specific time, after the usual trial period. As a second decade professional, you probably have more opportunities for this kind of referral than younger job seekers.

• *People from social/religious organizations*. Church, synagogue, lodge or club members, sports groups like bowling leagues or golfing buddies are ripe for networking.

• *College and postgraduate instructors*. Former professors, deans, administrators, advisors, and classmates all should be an important part of your networking life at this stage. Review your academic life to develop contacts for your search, particularly if you went to graduate school. Alumni association activities are another good way to expand your list. Your university may also offer ongoing placement services to its graduates.

• *Local professionals*. Bankers, real estate agents, lawyers, doctors, accountants, and others. Here's a call representative of one job seeker who went from an anonymous midlevel job he'd held for many years in a large company to a successful top management position at a smaller company—all because he picked up the telephone.

RECEPTIONIST: Good morning, Brophy and Associates, Certified Public Accountants.

MARK: Good morning. I'd like to speak to Dean Brophy, please. This is Mark Gibson calling.

RECEPTIONIST: One moment, Mr. Gibson.

DEAN: Mark! Good morning. I didn't expect to hear from you until tax season—is there something I can do for you?

MARK: As a matter of fact, Dean, there is. You know when we got together earlier this year, I told you I went back to school to complete my MBA? My job as an engineer had stalled, and I saw the MBA as an effective way to give my career a boost.

DEAN: I remember. How's it going?

MARK: Well, it's been a long haul, but I'm almost ready to graduate and I'm organizing my job search. When we talked, you mentioned that a client—a small steel company—was in need of reorganization. Do you think they could use a structural engineer with an MBA from a good school to help streamline them? My concentration is in finance, and I have a lot of steel experience.

DEAN: I'm glad you called. We're just about to pull together a new management team. I'd forgotten our last conversation, but your qualifications might be just what we need. How about if you and I get together and talk this week, and then we'll arrange to meet with the client. Can you be here Thursday at 4 o'clock?

MARK: I'll be there. I'll stop by today and drop off my resume for you to review in the meantime.

DEAN: Great. I'm looking forward to it, Mark. There's a lot of potential at this company, but it needs direction to get where it belongs.

MARK: I already have some ideas. Let's discuss them Thursday and take it from there. I'll see you then.

DEAN: Good enough. Bye.

MARK: Goodbye.

Your personal contacts will continue to grow as each lead branches off into others. Get in touch with all of them and record their "trail." You'll need it—now and in the future.

Networking Current Business Associates

You need a modicum of finesse with the variety of people who fall into this category. First a caveat: Consider these names especially carefully. What you don't want is a stab in the back from someone whom you consider an ally, only to find out she's been coveting your job and can't wait to pass on your little secret to the boss.

How to Proceed With Your Best Prospects

▪ *Infiltrate the secretarial "secret service."* As I noted in a previous book,

Even in the smallest companies, the secretaries call the shots. . . . Their responsibilities, knowledge, influence with their bosses and constant communication with each other make them extremely powerful. . . .

Secretaries are continuously exposed to the latest rumors and gossip, which gives them the opportunity to detect changes long before they occur. The sources of the information are other secretaries who prepare the correspondence, organization charts, personnel status changes, job requisitions, termination notices, final checks, and the myriad other documents that affect your job.

To infiltrate, you must make your secretary your official secret agent. Listen carefully to her observations. Don't forget her birthday or other personally important events. The rewards will more than pay for the cost of flowers during Secretary's Week (the third week of April). Rewards go a long way to engendering the loyalty that keeps you abreast of major decisions inside the company, and possibly what's happening on the outside, too.

▪ *Invite yourself to join the in crowd.* In high school, these were called cliques. If you thought them impenetrable in school, perhaps you avoid them at work. Not wise.

Recognizing their inherent power base makes it obvious why you need to cultivate them. Watch when certain employees:

- Constantly meet with the boss and others above him.
- Receive a particular office, preferential assignments, seminar approvals, reimbursement, and more smiles from supervisors.
- Have similar ages, religions, political views, opinions, speech patterns, vocabularies, eating and drinking habits, and ways of dressing.
- Cluster together at breaks and other times they are off duty.
- Are promoted or get raises faster for no apparent reason.

There are other signals, but these are enough to define the clique. Infiltration is just a matter of imitation. You don't have to change your entire belief system.

Align yourself with several cliques, even if they oppose each other. Steel yourself to break through their initial stares, then actively listen, and agree when you can. Strange as it sounds, an open mind is often the entry into a clique.

But you must make the first move. Start by saying, "Do you mind if I join you for lunch?" Although inappropriate with your boss, you can (and should) use the lunch hour for developing a bond with coworkers. Consider going out twice a week with influential members of a clique. Shared outside experiences help break down barriers, and once your coalition develops, you'll pick up a lot of valuable information.

▪ *Align with the company-liners.* A variation of an in-crowd is a group of employees known as *company-liners.* They wear service pins and display company awards in their offices. Company-liners often become senior executives because they internalize company goals, communicate them to their staffs, and execute corporate policy. To get into this crowd, you should:

▪ Openly stress the importance of "doing a good job." Use company slogans, if they exist.
▪ Extol the virtues of the company.
▪ Suggest ways to improve operations wherever possible (reducing costs, increasing efficiency, developing new products, etc.).
▪ Never publicly criticize anything about the management or direction of the company.

Although you may inwardly rebel at such toadying, aligning with or at least acknowledging this group's existence will increase the likelihood of long-term employment with regular promotions. These are not the people with whom to share your plans to leave, but they can be useful in seeing which way the wind blows in your company. What you learn from them can help you determine whether to stay or go.

▪ *Cultivate current business contacts.* These contacts include customers, vendors, and consultants to your current employer. Those who rely on your company's business may not want to talk as readily, but developing a relationship with key people in these companies can provide valuable insights and job leads.

Include major players from these and other sources on your *get-work network.* In your conversations, ask for advice and guidance, and the opportunity to show your resume "because I've always valued your opinion." Don't do the "I'm looking. Do you know of something?" routine. If they know something, they'll get your meaning.

▪ *Be kind to strangers (the business variety).* Some of the best business relationships on earth began midair in an airplane. Even more began at an airport waiting gate, the van to a hotel, and inside its lobby. When two business travelers exchange business cards, global networking occurs. It is good to have friends in all places—near and far.

What to Do With Your Leads

Once you've prepared your complete contact list, give it an initial run through.

■ *Make an initial call.* If you're uncertain what to say, you can even prepare a miniscript. It might sound like this:

> "Hi, Tom. This is Greg Jenkins. [If Tom remembers you, fine. If not, you may have to rekindle memories.] You recall I was in the office next to yours in purchasing at Hutchins Manufacturing, a couple of years ago. [Anticipate a moment or two of catching up and small talk. Then get to the business at hand.] I'm beginning to look for new opportunities since I seem to have risen as far as possible at Warner-Green. If you can refer me to someone who might be interested in a purchasing supervisor or v.p. slot, I'd sure like to know about it. [More than likely, since you've been quite specific, they will not immediately know of anything. So you continue.] Listen, I'd just like you to keep your eyes and ears open if anything looks promising, or if you hear that someone is expanding their purchasing department."

Another variation may go something like this:

> "Bob, it's Tina. I know it's been awhile since our Cousins' Club got together, and we really should do something about it soon. Anyway, the reason for my call is that I remember that the last time we did get together, you mentioned that your brother-in-law had just opened a new natural foods store. How's he doing? You know, I'm planning on changing from Great Superfoods and would like to get into a smaller operation with room for growth. Do you think you could mention me to him?

You get the idea. The permutations on these conversations are endless, but they lead to the same goal: get your contacts to stay alert for possibilities on your behalf. Be sure to tell them you'll be pleased to reciprocate.

■ *Send a resume and cover letter to each of your primary contacts.* Once through your list, you'll have determined which names to omit. Assume all the rest are primary contacts. In the letter remind them of your conversation and reiterate the general position you're looking for. Don't focus your job target too narrowly; that's one reason your resume should not have an objective on it. By the same token, being too specific about your job title or goal may unnecessarily restrict your contacts' creative thoughts. Let them get the feel of what you want. What's most important is to stress you'd be interested in talking with anyone who may have a viable lead. Tell each contact what you've done before and what you can do in the future; this can give them insights into possibilities they might otherwise never have thought of for you. Offer assistance in any way possible.

■ *Always ask permission to use your contact's name.* Then do so on the phone and in written correspondence. Names are like gold. They shine with star referral quality. Always open your conversation with a phrase such as,

> "Susan Johnson at Selby Office Products suggested I contact you."

In the remainder of the conversation, briefly summarize who you are and why you're making the contact. End the conversation or letter with a statement suggesting a visit or further call to discuss mutually beneficial plans.

■ *When you arrange a meeting be specific about the length of time it will take.* For an exploratory session, normally it should be no more than fifteen to twenty minutes. Be prepared with a list of questions. Don't overstay your allotted time, unless your contact urges you to do so.

■ *At a meeting arranged by a contact, it is imperative that you make the best presentation possible.* Some of these sessions may not pan out, but you can't afford to be anything less than superbly gracious. Today's nonproductive lead may later turn into tomorrow's excellent interview.

■ *"Pyramid" to maximize your contacts.* Ask each person you contact if they, in turn, know someone who may have additional information about your field. This technique works best for positions up to midlevel management. For senior slots, what counts are personal recommendations from one associate to another.

■ *At the end of the call, leave 'em with a smile.* Say something like, "I really appreciate the help you've given me. Here's my number, in case I can return the favor one day." This is a gesture of class. Say that you hope to see him or her soon, and, if appropriate (you'll be able to tell), follow up with an invitation for drinks or dinner.

■ *The most important element of networking is follow-up.* Try to get each contact to determine a follow-up time. Then adhere to it and recontact each person within the agreed-upon time. Be sure to report back quickly when a lead they've suggested pans out. They'll be delighted they were able to help. Always send a short, personalized thank-you note. Because a career is a long-time proposition, for maximum networking benefits, reestablish the contact once every year. Exhibit 13-1 is a simple form you can use to track your contacts on a note pad or file cards. It's also adaptable for your home computer.

Other Sources of Leads

Job Clubs

Self-help organizations for executives or professionals abound nationwide. Most have meetings, newsletters listing job openings, and resume exchanges. Some have job juries that critique your resume before its final printing. It can be very helpful to polish a resume aided and abetted by a jury of your peers.

Some organizations target specific populations such as the nationwide Forty Plus Clubs. Others focus on specific professions or career fields, for example, aerospace engineers in Southern California. Some are full-scale, profit-driven groups. Others are informal, voluntary, job-sharing clubs. Obviously, the values of the leads may vary widely.

Look at the job market publications discussed in Chapter 5 for names in your area. Call and ask about their service, practices, and

Exhibit 13-1. Contact results sheet.

Original Contact Date	Name and Title	Referred Me To	Results of Referral	Recontact On

fees. Then request a copy of their brochure, application form, and a recent newsletter to see if joining is worthwhile for you.

Trade Associations

Meetings of professional associations are rife with contact possibilities; after all, everyone there has the same general interests. Whether you decide to join a trade organization or merely opt for guest status at a few meetings, don't sit silently through the program and then leave. That's a sheer waste of money.

Network the members before and after the meeting. If it's a dinner event, get there early and try to canvas the room. When it's time for dinner, you can select a table where your best prospects have clustered and spend some quality time with them before the program.

Don't overlook the guest speaker. Many people will converge on him or her once the program is over, but you can hang back and wait until the crush thins. Be sure to comment positively on some aspect of the presentation. Then offer your business card and ask for the speaker's. Say something such as, "I'd like to call you to discuss some areas I'm interested in." Leave it at that.

When you make the call, you can remind him or her where you met. Bring up your job search and background in a sentence or two (no more) and ask if they have any thoughts about someone you might call. The better known the speaker, the more difficult it may be to get past his gatekeeper. Use such statements as "I met Jack Mackenzie at the Public Relations Society's meeting last week and he suggested I call him."

If you decide to join the organization, don't be a passive member. A writer friend of mine belonged to a local writer's group for eight years before she decided to actively participate. Nothing happened in spite of her listing in the group's annual directory. Within six months of the time she volunteered to work on and subsequently direct the association's telephone job hotline, she had several major assignments under her belt, including two book contracts.

Another two benefits from membership: You'll stay current in your field, and your dues and related expenses are tax deductible.

You can find notices of meetings in trade journals. Local papers may also run them on their business pages. Visit the library and look up your specialty in *The Encyclopedia of Associations*. You'll be amazed at the wealth of valuable information it contains, directly relating to your career interests.

If you live nearby when the national association of your trade specialty convenes, or if you're really motivated to spend the money for airfare and hotel, you can dramatically increase your leads. National career authorities estimate you can net forty to fifty contacts within a two- to three-day span. From early morning coffees to post-dinner get-togethers, it's a networking cornucopia.

If there's a related trade exhibition, visit the booths to collect company materials. You can use them for background information, so that when you call your newly made contacts, you'll have something relevant to say about their companies.

Collect business cards like mad. In your hotel room, write notes on the back to jog your memory. Back home, immediately write letters, recalling conversations. List your achievements with quick-reading bullets, and include your resume. Call back and ask if they've read your resume. Chances are they haven't. Repeat your qualifications and politely ask if they have a contact that you might call.

Trade shows and conferences are also an excellent place to meet editors of journals related to your field. Often, such a publication may sponsor the event and will likely have a booth on the convention floor.

Get a copy of the publication, read it, and introduce yourself to the editor. Say something like "I read Article X and feel the rundown you did on the industry is long overdue." Whatever you say, make it obvious that you have looked closely at the publication. Then ask for her card.

Once at home, give her a call. Ask first if she's on deadline. If she's not, she may want to tap into your knowledge of the industry and the two of you can be off to a productive friendship. As a journalist, she may not refer you to her private contacts or sources, but with her industrywide knowledge, she may point you in the direction of a promising company.

Community Groups

Interview leads can also be as close as Main Street in your own hometown. You don't have to own a business to attend a chamber of commerce mixer. Similarly, you can affiliate with Rotary, Jaycees, or other groups that were networking nonstop before the term was invented. Make sure that these organizations will sufficiently pay off in leads before making a longtime commitment.

In some cities, the chamber of commerce conducts job forums, either on their own or together with service organizations or sales executives clubs. Often they may charge a nominal fee.

Many colleges and universities also offer short one- or two-session noncredit extension courses that cater to like-minded professionals. Call your local college and ask for a catalogue that lists classes, times, and prices. By attending one or more such sessions, you can further expand your contacts with others on your career path.

The broader your professional contacts, the more quickly you'll acquire the vital information that is the lifeblood of career progress. Building relationships with people who can help you (and you can help in return, of course) is critical to your long-range career success.

Chapter 14

Keeping Your Job Until You're Ready to Leave

Ongoing job market research gives you a low-risk commonsense way to evaluate your present position. It also arms you with facts that can be used either to negotiate more effectively with your employer for promotions and/or raises or to move quickly and efficiently if you decide to leave.

If things at your present employer seem off kilter—more closed-door, top-level meetings, empty desks, a freeze or reduction in hiring, for example—you might want to check with one of your friendly know-all power bases. Whatever the news, he or she will know. Roaming around human relations or benefits departments with payroll or benefits questions is another clue. Are they open or distracted?

Once you've compared the market out there with your own position, if you decide to move on, remember one thing: When you're employed you're always in a stronger position with prospective employers.

Current Employment = Greater Attractiveness

Potential employers are generally much more receptive to job seekers who are currently employed. From the new employer's standpoint, you're more attractive if someone else thinks you're worth the salary. Chapter 12 discussed headhunters. You're also more attractive to them as an employed candidate.

These placement services are your best source of referrals when you're employed, since they can present your qualifications in much the same way as a public relations representative does. They display you in the most professional light by emphasizing your current responsibilities. While you're working, they can chase down leads you'd otherwise never know about. They possess three things you don't: knowledge of the current job market, contacts, and time. Working together while you're employed is the best way to form a valuable, productive alliance.

Current Employment = Greater Negotiating Leverage

Because you're presently employed, the prospective employer knows you have another secure option—to stay where you are.

When you speak to an interviewer, your approach to phone conversations and interviews should be that you are being paid to do a job, and it would be improper for you to take company time for personal business. Besides, you have a lot of responsibilities to your present employer and want to be as effective as possible.

You get the picture: Use your integrity and stature as a basis for special treatment in employment interview scheduling for evenings or weekends. You'll get it, too. Why? Because you're just a little hard to get!

Creating Counteroffers

There are times when having word leak back to your current employer about your job search can even be beneficial. More than one executive has been given a promotion and/or salary increase when the company found they were about to lose him or her.

Using this ploy you should attempt to persuade the decision makers in your company that you are extremely eager and able to move up. If you've been there for a number of years, they may be taking you for granted. With the possibility of losing "good old dependable Joe" may come better negotiating leverage than you'd otherwise have.

Preparation for Separation

One American changes a job every twenty seconds, six or more times in the average lifetime, and the rate is increasing as we near the next millennium. In spite of these figures, most people don't take proper steps while they're on the job to maximize their negotiating power when they're about to leave. Why? It's like buying an umbrella:

There's no need for it when the sun is shining, and you can't find one when it's raining.

Doing your corporate homework before you're ready to leave can give you an obvious objective edge: You will have all your facts neatly together. You can present a coherent rationale for (a) leaving—so the company can present options to retain your services or (b) keeping you—even if the company is going through downsizing.

In addition, being prepared also gives you an important subjective advantage: the attitude of a winner.

Developing a Separation File

You should immediately prepare three pairs of legal size manila file folders with two pronged fasteners on the top of each side just like lawyers use. The labels of each pair should be identical, since one is for originals (where available) and the other is for copies. The labels should be typed carefully, all in capital letters:

> (your full name including middle initial) v. the full name of your employer)

Then, on the front of each pair of original and duplicate folders, approximately one inch below the tab, place labels, also typed in capital letters, with one of these words: *correspondence, evidence,* and *chronology.*

Gathering Evidence to Use

1. *Correspondence file.* On the left side, place all letters (recommendations, favorable customer letters, etc.). On the right side, place all company memoranda (related to any progress in which you were involved or other favorable references). The earliest should be at the bottom, and the dates should be in order so that the most recent document is on the top.

2. *Evidence file.* Clip any pay stubs, telephone messages, promotion announcements, bulletins, newspaper articles, laws, pictures, or other significant items on the left side. Put your employment agreement (if any), job descriptions, relevant pages from the employee handbook and procedure manual, performance review forms, and

any other items you think you might need for future use on the right side.

3. *Chronology file.* This file is the best of all. It belongs on the right side. On legal size paper prepare a form that looks like the one shown in Exhibit 14-1. Photocopy ten pages or so for your use. Then enter any occurrences that could be used in the future to enhance your bargaining position. Potential entries include favorable remarks by

Exhibit 14-1. Job chronology form.

Job Chronology		Page No.
Date	*Initials*	*Notes*

senior managers, promises that weren't kept, changes in your job classification without letting you know, job achievements, and so forth. Once you get used to doing this, you'll be amazed how the number of pages on the right side increases. Initial each entry, even though you are the only one doing the entering, since it will look more authentic.

These files should never be taken to your office. They remain safely at home where additional information is to be inserted in the evening, and where they are ready for use when needed. One or two blank chronology forms should be in your attache case (or locked desk) for completion when you have enough privacy. Try not to wait until the evening, since you'll tend to forget the details and you may want to forget the whole episode! You'll also be busy and tired. Just be sure to file the information the same evening you bring it home. Periodically update the duplicate files by photocopying the originals, unless you were able to do so before you brought them home. The only other item you need is a yellow legal pad.

Surviving Downsizing

Now, you're ready to move into action should the downsize ax drop. Here's a worst-case scenario.

It's midweek. You're at your desk working away when your boss buzzes and asks you to come into his office. When you enter, he asks you to close the door and sit down. He has "The Book" (your personnel file) inscribed with your name, closed on his desk. After a few anxious minutes, he tells you that he's afraid he has bad news for you. He may say it's a "downsize," "layoff," or "cutback." Then again, he may tell you that he has to let you go or that you're fired. There are many other ways to say it, but your response should always be the same:

> You: What's the reason?
> Boss: We're downsizing, and the quality of your work hasn't been up to standards.
> You: When is this effective?
> Boss: Right away.
> You: I had no idea this was going to happen. Can we discuss it tomorrow morning?
> Boss: I'm sorry, but it's effective now.
> You: I understand, but I'm really in a state of shock. Of course, I'll leave now, but I'd like to meet you again in the morning.

Boss: I can't do it until tomorrow afternoon at 2 o'clock. Why don't you sign this receipt for your final checks?

You: I'd like to see them, but I don't want to sign anything now. I'll be here tomorrow at two. I can clean out my things and say a few goodbyes then.

Boss: All right. Again, I'm sorry.

You: See you tomorrow at two.

Boss: Fine.

Now, go *directly* home avoiding as many other employees as you can. Then pull out your files. If the duplicates are not updated, go directly to the nearest photocopy center and make a complete set of all three duplicate files. Put the duplicate set into your attache case.

Now, you can make any "downsize duty" phone calls to members of your family and friends. Limit the number and make them brief, however. You've got things to do and you're not going to take this lying down.

Next, call the local labor law enforcement agency and attempt to speak to a staff attorney or senior official. Tell her your circumstances, ask for advice on the law and procedure for filing a claim, and listen. Take notes. Then call the local unemployment office with the same routine. It's possible unlawful discrimination or wrongful termination has occurred. You should get a sense of that from your discussions. If there's still time that afternoon, keep gathering and writing down as much information as you can. That evening, review your notes and outline your objectives for the meeting. Use one sheet of paper for each objective. For example, you might want to obtain:

- Reinstatement
- Retention on the payroll for an interim period
- Use of an office, a telephone, and clerical services
- Payment of outplacement consulting services
- Severance pay
- Holiday pay
- Unemployment benefits
- Reference letters
- Eligibility for rehire
- Maintenance of group insurance
- Vesting in the retirement plan

Number them in order of priority and work on the most important one first, writing out the reasons it is justified. Use the information in your files, and organize the duplicates so you can find them readily. On your legal pad just list the items the same way, one per page (but with no notes). Then get as much rest as you can that evening, and use the phone the next morning to call the government agents back or start looking for a job.

Go to the meeting dressed in dark, conservative clothes, with your attache case containing the correspondence and evidence duplicate files (never take the originals since they can be lost or seized), and your legal pad with the headings. Use them as needed. The duplicate chronology file and your recent handwritten notes should not be used now. (They may be used later, if you press on with a suit.) If you take them, leave them in your car or somewhere else outside the facility.

Then, simply go through your list, make notes on the legal pad under the proper heading, and see what you can negotiate.

You've used the element of surprise to your advantage, maximized your time to organize your thoughts, used the information you gathered, and brought a few intimidation tools into the meeting (your clothes, attache case, correspondence and evidence files, and legal pad). The original files and your notes can be used if you wish to pursue the matter further.

It may never get this bad. But it doesn't hurt to be prepared. By being prepared for the worst, you're actually helping to ensure the best—the best for the next, most prosperous decade of your career.

Chapter 15

Conclusion

You've come full circle. We began with that vague sense of unease about your current prospects and ended with you facing the worst demons of downsizing yet still ending up a winner. There is no mystery about what to do next. In my multiple decades as career counselor and employment attorney I've seen the basic techniques in this book work again and again.

If you're feeling uncertain, the best way to overcome negativism is by positive programming. If you find yourself procrastinating about improvement, begin by making a small financial commitment. Subscribe to one of the trade magazines, attend one or two networking meetings from professional or civic organizations, or enroll in a skills training program.

This will help you overcome the most difficult phase—initial inertia against making any change. The early steps of self-development are the most difficult; by making a modest resolution you can live up to, you'll soon be able to see tangible improvements. This may keep you on the right path:

> During a recent book promotion tour, I found myself in front of a microphone on an all-night radio talk show, just outside New York City. I'd been on this tour for two weeks and was dizzy with fatigue. During a commercial, I told the host I'd have to be leaving soon, since I had to catch a plane.
>
> The host announced that the next call would be the last. The caller asked, "What does J.D. and C.P.C. after your name mean?"
>
> Of course the straight answer would have been Juris Doctor and Certified Placement Counselor. But I just couldn't be straight under the circumstances.
>
> As I stood up and began to remove my headset, my candid reply said it all. "J.D. stands for 'Just do it' [Mind you, this way w-a-y before Nike began using the slogan!] and C.P.C. stands for 'courage, perseverance, and confidence.' "

Those phrases should be the watchwords of your upcoming job search campaign. Remember, it's not how qualified you are. It's how important employers think you are. Armed with your newly acquired knowledge, they just can't do without you!

Bibliography

Periodicals

Groves, Martha. "PC Users Find It's Not PC to Use Nerd Word," *Los Angeles Times* (November 2, 1993), pp. D1, D18.

Henkoff, Ronald. "Winning the Career Game," *Fortune* (July 12, 1992), pp. 34–36, 40–41, 44–64.

Laut, David. "Firm Find That Employee Perks Return Big Bonuses," *Los Angeles Times* (October 25, 1993), pp. A1, A14.

Pollan, Stephen M., and Mark Levine. "You Are Your Own Business," *Working Woman* (September 1993), pp. 50, 103, 105, 107.

"The 25 Hottest Careers—Jobs Built to Last," *Working Woman* (July 1992), pp. 45–51.

"Aging of America," *Life* (1993), p. 36.

Books

Allen, Jeffrey G., and Jess Gorkin. *Finding the Right Job at Midlife* (New York: Simon & Schuster, 1985).

Allen, Jeffrey G. *Jeff Allen's Best: Get the Interview, Get the interview* (New York: John Wiley, 1990).

Allen, Jeffrey G. *Jeff Allen's Best: The Resume* (New York: John Wiley, 1988).

Allen, Jeffrey G. *Jeff Allen's Best: Win the Job* (New York: John Wiley, 1990).

Allen, Jeffrey G. *Surviving Corporate Downsizing: How to Keep Your Job* (New York: John Wiley, 1988).

Asher, Donald. *The Overnight Job Change Strategy*, Berkeley, Calif.: Ten Speed Press, 1993).

Bardwick, Judith. *The Plateauing Trap* (New York: AMACOM, 1986).

Birsner, E. Patricia. *The Forty-Plus Job Hunting Guide* (New York: Facts on File, 1990).

Bloch, Deborah P. *How to Have a Winning Job Interview* (Lincolnwood, Ill.: NTC Publishing Group, 1992).

Cohen, Herb. *You Can Negotiate Anything* (New York: Bantam, 1990).

Connaroe, Richard. *Executive Search* (New York: Van Nostrand Reinhold, 1976.

Cowle, Jerry. *How to Survive Getting Fired—And Win* (Chicago: Follett's, 1979).

Dawson, Kenneth, and Sheryl Dawson. *Job Search: The Total System* (New York: John Wiley, 1988).

Deep, Sam, and Lyle Sussman. Smart Moves (Redding, Mass.: Addison-Wesley, 1990).

Donough, Donald L. *The Middle Years* (New York: Holt, Rinehart & Winston, 1981).

Gerberg, Robert. *Robert Gerberg's Job Changing System* (Kansas City, Mo.: Andrews & McMeel, 1986).

Graen, George B. *Unwritten Rules for Your Career* (New York: John Wiley, 1989).

Goldstein, Ross, with Diana Landau. *Fortysomething: Claiming the Passion of Your Midlife Years* (Los Angeles: Jeremy P. Tarcher, 1990).

Jameson, Robert. *The Professional Job Changing System* (Kansas City, Mo.: Andrews & McMeel, 1976).

Jarvik, Lissy, and Gary Small. *Parentcare—A Common Sense Guide for Adult Children* (New York: Crown Publishers, 1988).

Kennedy, Joyce Lain and Thomas J. Morrow. *Electronic Resume Revolution* (New York: John Wiley, 1994).

Kinder, Melvyn. *Going Nowhere Fast* (Manassas Park, Va.: Impact Publications, 1993).

Krannich, Caryl Rae, and Ronald L. Krannich. *Job Search Letters That Get Results* (Manassas Park, Va.: Impact Publications, 1992).

Lee, Nancy. *Targeting the Top* (New York: Doubleday, 1980).

Smith, Donald G. . . . *And They Also Kick You When You're Down* (New York: Dodd, Mead & Co., 1988).

Strasser, Stephen, and John Sena. *Transitions* (Englewood Cliffs, N.J.: Prentice Hall, 1988).

Waitley, Denis. *The Psychology of Winner* (New York: Berkley Publishing, 1984).

Witt, Melanie Astaire. *Job Strategies for People With Disabilities* (Princeton, N.J.: Peterson's Guides, 1992).

Yate, Martin. *Knock 'Em Dead* (Holbrook, Mass.: Bob Adams, 1992).

Zunin, Leonard, and Natalie Zunin. *Contact: The First Four Minutes* (New York: Ballantine, 1973).

Index

About the Author

Jeffrey G. Allen, J.D., C.P.C., is America's foremost employment attorney. For almost a decade, Mr. Allen was an executive recruiter and a human resources manager. This direct experience has been coupled with his employment law practice for the past 20 years. As a certified placement counselor, certified employment specialist, and professional negotiator, Mr. Allen is considered the nation's leading authority on resume preparation.

Mr. Allen is the author of more best-selling books in the employment field than anyone else. Among them are *How to Turn an Interview Into a Job, Finding the Right Job at Midlife, The Employee Termination Handbook, The Placement Strategy Handbook, Placement Management, The Complete Q&A Job Interview Book, The Perfect Job Reference, The Perfect Follow-Up Method to Get the Job,* the popular three book series *Jeff Allen's Best,* and most recently, *The Resume Makeover.* He writes a nationally syndicated column entitled "Placements and The Law," conducts seminars, and is regularly featured in television, radio, and newspaper interviews.

Mr. Allen has served as director of the National Placement Law Center, Special Advisor to the American Employment Association and General Counsel to the California Association of Personnel Consultants.